COLLAGE CARDS

45 GREAT GREETINGS!

Martingale®
& C O M P A N Y

Collage Cards: 45 Great Greetings!
© 2004 by Martingale & Company®

Martingale®
& C O M P A N Y

Martingale & Company
20205 144th Avenue NE
Woodinville, WA 98072-8478
www.martingale-pub.com

Printed in China
09 08 07 06 05 04   8 7 6 5 4 3 2 1

Library of Congress Cataloging-in-Publication data available upon request.

ISBN 1-56477-541-0

CREDITS

PRESIDENT: *Nancy J. Martin*

CEO: *Daniel J. Martin*

PUBLISHER: *Jane Hamada*

EDITORIAL DIRECTOR: *Mary V. Green*

MANAGING EDITOR: *Tina Cook*

TECHNICAL EDITOR: *Candie Frankel*

COPY EDITOR: *Linda Smith*

DESIGN DIRECTOR: *Stan Green*

ILLUSTRATOR: *Laurel Strand*

COVER DESIGNER: *Shelly Garrison*

TEXT DESIGNER: *Rose Sheifer*

PHOTOGRAPHER: *Bill Lindner*

MISSION STATEMENT
Dedicated to providing quality products and service to inspire creativity.

CONTENTS

INTRODUCTION

People love to give and receive greeting cards. Cards offer a thoughtful, affordable way to convey a personal message. If you've ever browsed through the racks at a card shop, you know that there are cards for just about anything you could want to say. Yet despite the vast array, sometimes it's hard to find a card that's exactly right for the person or the occasion.

Making your own greeting cards offers a way out of this conundrum. You can use beautiful art papers, scrapbooking supplies, photographs, rubber stamps, buttons, ribbons, and other decorative items to create a unique card that will be fun to receive and display. If you loved doing arts and crafts projects as a child but can't find time in your adult schedule for imaginative play, card making can help you reenter your creative zone. Most cards can be made in 30 minutes or less. Think of each card as a mini multimedia collage, waiting for your personal contribution.

Collage Cards offers a collection of more than 40 card projects that you can make for holidays, birthdays, and other personal milestones. Each project includes a materials list and step-by-step instructions. You can make the cards exactly as pictured, or you can try combining ideas and techniques from several cards to come up with your own designs. If you are new to card making (or if you need a quick refresher course), be sure to read through "Card-Making Basics" beginning on page 5. Here you will find all you need to know to get your collage card studio up and running.

CARD-MAKING BASICS

The collage approach to card making is a bit like buying lunch at a cafeteria. You pick out the items you want and leave the rest for another day. Every collage card pulls together various elements that contribute shape, color, texture, and contrast to the design. Let's tour the card-making cafeteria and take a closer look at the different media you will be using.

PAPER

A key element in any card is the paper. A paper can be stiff or pliable, thick or thin, smooth or rough. Part of the pleasure of receiving and opening a handmade card is the experience of handling one or more specialty papers. Think of it as a visit to a hands-on gallery, where you not only view but can also touch the works of art. Card making lets you pick and choose exquisite papers right off the art store cafeteria line.

Good choices for the card itself are cardstock, handmade paper, drawing paper, and watercolor paper. All come in colors, except watercolor paper, which is white or cream. Cardstock is stiff and comes in matte and shiny finishes. Vellum is extremely thin and translucent and sets an elegant tone. All of these paper types can be layered over one another in various ways to build a design.

Other paper products you can collage include stickers, self-adhesive mesh, tags, tissue paper, corrugated paper, and small envelopes. Maps, gift wrap, and papers printed for scrapbooking give you pattern options. For random text, you might try a page torn from an old book.

Folding Paper

Use a "score and fold" approach to make clean, professionally creased folds in your cards. Scoring compresses the fibers in the paper and sets a path for the fold line. Begin by aligning a thick clear acrylic grid ruler on the paper at the desired fold line. Press down on the ruler with one hand. Use your other hand to draw a bone folder against the edge of the ruler, lightly denting, or scoring, the paper as you go (fig. 1). Now fold the paper on the scored line. Rub the smooth side of the bone folder over the folded edge to set the crease (fig. 2).

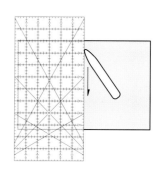

Fig. 1

Fig. 2

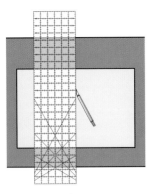

Fig. 3

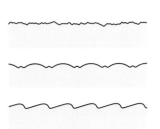

Fig. 4

Fig. 5

Cutting Paper

Various tools can be used to cut paper and cardstock. For a clean edge, use an X-Acto knife or a rotary cutter. Lay the paper on a self-healing cutting mat. Align a thick acrylic grid ruler on top of the paper. Press down on the ruler to hold it in place and then draw the knife or rotary blade against the ruler edge to make the cut (fig. 3). The ruler's built-in grid can help you measure and cut in one step. Another option for cutting is a small paper cutter with a gridded bed.

For random cuts or short straight cuts, use scissors. Specialty scissors and edgers let you create deckled, scalloped, and pinked edges (fig. 4). To make a decoratively cut edge, draw a faint guideline with a pencil and then cut along the line with an edger. You can also cut along a previously cut straight edge.

Small, perfectly round holes are made with a punch. A ¼" hole punch is a familiar office supply; for smaller holes, use a ⅛" punch. An "anywhere" punch allows you to punch holes in places where a conventional hole punch will not reach. Punches that cut squares, stars, hearts, and other simple silhouettes are also available (fig. 5). You can use the actual cutout shape or the framed negative shape.

For very small holes, use a paper piercer. Prepierced holes are easier to sew through by hand if you want to add decorative threads or beads—you won't crumple the paper as you try to insert your sewing needle. Pierced holes also look nice on their own.

A perforating blade makes tiny sequential cuts, or perforations. Perforated shapes are easy to punch out, or you can simply use the perforated lines decoratively.

Tearing Paper

You can tear one or more edges of a paper shape to resemble the deckle edge on a handmade paper. Tearing gives paper shapes a sophisticated, artsy appearance. A torn edge can be straight or freeform.

To tear a straight edge, place a clear acrylic grid ruler on the paper. Press down on the ruler and simultaneously lift up the exposed paper, pulling it gently toward you. For a more random tear, omit the ruler. Random tears made on the paper grain will be straighter than those made against the grain.

Templates

Some projects include actual-size template patterns. To make a template, place template plastic over the printed pattern and trace the pattern outline using a pencil. Use a ruler to draft straight lines accurately. Cut out the shape on the marked outline, using scissors for curves and an X-Acto knife and ruler for straight edges.

To use a plastic template, place it on the selected paper. The see-through quality of the plastic makes it possible to position the template on a particular area of a patterned paper or over a stamped image. Once the template is positioned, hold down the template with the fingers of one hand and use your other hand to trace around the outer edge with a pencil. Cut out the paper shape, once again using scissors or an X-Acto knife and ruler, as appropriate.

Plastic templates are ideal for marking and cutting multiples of the same shape. Unlike cardboard templates, they won't deteriorate after a few tracings. Always save your plastic templates for future projects. You can use them again and again.

RUBBER STAMPING

Rubber stamps let you add flat as well as embossed images to your cards quickly and easily. There are rubber stamps for every conceivable theme and interest. Alphabet stamps in uppercase and lowercase letters let you print simple messages. There are also stamps for printing borders and decorative designs.

In addition to rubber stamps, you will need an inkpad. You can use either a dye-based ink or a pigment ink to create a stamped image. Dye-based inks dry quickly after being stamped. Pigment inks stay wet longer and are used for embossing. Both types come in different colors.

How to Stamp Images

To ink your stamp, press it down on the inkpad several times. To print the image, set your inked stamp onto the paper and apply even pressure. Occasionally, a stamp will require gentle rocking to produce a complete print. Do a few test stampings on scrap paper to get the feel of each stamp you use.

To avoid smudging, keep your fingertips clean as you work and do not touch your project paper more than necessary. If a stamped image starts losing clarity after multiple stampings, blot the excess ink off the stamp with a damp paper towel and begin again. Be sure to clean and dry your stamps thoroughly when you are finished to keep them in good condition. Professional stamp cleaning supplies are available for this purpose.

Centering a stamped image on a precut piece of paper can be tricky. If eyeballing the placement doesn't work for you, stamp on a larger piece of paper to start and then cut the paper to the desired size around the image.

Embossing

You can use rubber stamps and embossing powders to create embossed, or raised, images. Embossing powders are available in a range of colors, textures, and finishes that add interest and dimension to card projects. For the best results, choose simple images without a lot of fine details.

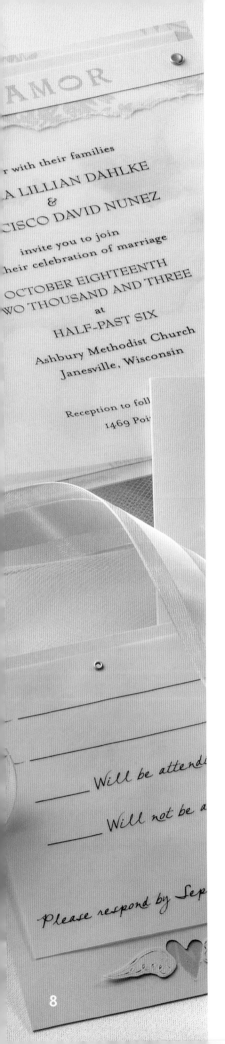

Stamp the image using a pigment ink or a special heat embossing ink. Sprinkle embossing powder over the wet inked surface, let it dry for a minute or so, and then tap off the excess powder. Funnel the excess powder back into its container for reuse. (This part of the process may remind you of the glue-and-glitter projects you did as a child.)

Examine the stamped paper carefully. If you see any stray particles of powder, remove them with a dry artist's brush. Use an electric heat tool to heat and melt the embossing powder. Heat tools made especially for embossing operate at just the right temperature to melt the powder in 20 to 30 seconds.

COMPUTERS AND PHOTOCOPIERS

Computers and photocopiers are useful tools for adding text and images to your cards. The more savvy you are with these machines, the more you will be able to accomplish. A key advantage is the capability of turning out multiple copies for large mailings, such as invitations or holiday cards, efficiently and economically. Visit a commercial photocopy and computer center, such as Kinko's, for printing and copying needs that you can't accomplish at home.

Working with Text

Text that is printed on a separate paper and affixed to the card creates a rich, layered look. Composing a detailed text, such as a wedding invitation or a birth announcement, is easy on a computer. Font choices, spacing, centering, and other software features are available at the touch of a button.

Create a file, type in your text, and make the necessary software selections. When you have a font, size, and layout that you like, do a test print of the file on plain paper. Measure the text printout area to see how it will fit on your card and make any needed adjustments. Typically, you will trim the printed sheet to the correct size for the card. A few tries are generally needed to fine-tune the text layout and trim size. If the printout area is small, see if you can fit the text for several cards on one sheet. You may also want to print and compare a few totally different layouts before making a final selection.

Once your file is perfect, do a test print on your project paper. If the paper is oversized, trim it to 8 1/2" x 11" to fit in your printer. If the paper has a distinct front and back, make sure it feeds into the printer correctly. Make a complete card using your test print. Once you have made a satisfactory prototype, go ahead and print the text for all of the cards.

Working with Images

A complete home computer setup places countless images at your fingertips. You can download copyright-free images from the Internet, scan drawings or photos, or upload family pictures from your digital camera. Use your computer software to resize the images as needed. You can also combine images and text from several different sources and print them as one file. Printing onto inkjet-printable canvas or clear transparency film gives you new media to work into your collage. As always, economize by fitting as many images as possible on each sheet.

Use the sepia-tone setting when copying fine artwork or photographs to retain the fine details and look of continuous tone photography. You will find you can print beautiful, quality pictures for your cards at a fraction of the cost of having actual duplicate photos made.

METAL ACCENTS

Hard, dimensional, and sometimes industrial-looking, metal accents play off the paper elements in a card. The contrast between the two media is especially appealing in cards designed for men. An easy way to include a metal/paper contrast in your projects is to use paper tags with metal rims.

Some metal findings are purely ornamental. These include wire spirals, charms, beaded chains, and chicken wire. Other metal findings, such as rivets and eyelets, can be functional as well as decorative.

There are two types of eyelets: those with holes and those without holes. Both types are attached to the card in the same way and can perform the function of riveting layers of paper together. Round hole eyelets can also serve as rings for tying on a tag or a few strands of fiber. Eyelets without holes are actually small charms. The part that shows on the card surface can be a word, a letter, or a shape, such as a snowflake or a heart. You can install several eyelet letters side by side to spell out a simple message.

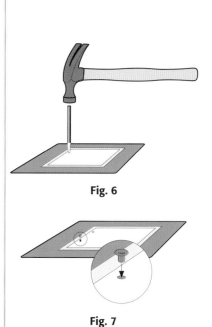

Fig. 6

Installing Eyelets

1. Layer the papers right side up and punch a hole at the appropriate spot. If you are using an "anywhere" punch, lay the papers flat on a cutting mat. Hold the punch perpendicular to the paper and tap with a hammer (fig. 6).

2. Insert the eyelet into the punched hole, front to back (fig. 7).

3. Turn the layered papers over. Make sure the eyelet prongs pass through the hole completely and that the papers are tightly layered (fig. 8).

4. Place an eyelet setter on top of the eyelet, perpendicular to the work surface. Tap with a hammer a couple of times to make the prongs flare out and roll down (fig. 9).

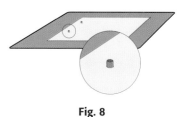

Fig. 7

Fig. 8

FIBERS AND THREADS

Fibers, even small amounts, can help establish your collage theme. A bit of hemp twine is perfect on a masculine birthday card for the fisherman. Crisp organdy ribbons create a festive, elegant air on a New Year's Eve invitation. Try shiny ribbons for a formal look, fuzzy yarns for a more casual,

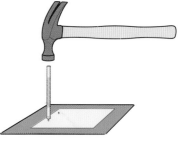

Fig. 9

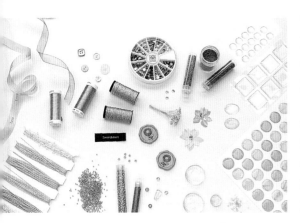

laid-back look. If you are making cards in multiples, buy ribbon by the yard or buy a ball of yarn. Otherwise, see if you can pick out odds and ends from your stash. There's no rule that says all your cards—even the "identical" ones—have to look alike.

Another fun way to add fiber to paper cards is with a sewing machine. Stitch right through the paper layers, using a contrasting sewing thread. If you drop the feed dogs on the machine, you can guide the card in circles or at random under the moving needle. The stitching will be whimsical, playful, and imprecise— just the ticket when you want a zany, artsy look.

BEADS AND STONES

Think of beads and stones as the jewelry on your collage. Glass rhinestones, plastic gemstones, sequins, and seed beads can add sparkle as well as dimension to the card surface. Buttons can serve a similar function. Fill large or awkward shapes with glitter glue to achieve a similar effect.

To magnify part of a text or picture, use page pebbles. These clear acrylic stones are flat on one side. Affix the flat side to the paper and then peer through the domed side to experience the magnifying effect.

ADHESIVES

Various adhesives are used in card making, depending on the materials being joined. Using two or more different adhesives in a collage card is the norm rather than the exception. It's a good idea to test your adhesives on scrap materials, especially when you are trying a new adhesive for the first time, to make sure the hold is secure.

Adhesive Tapes

Adhesive tapes are used to join one paper to another. Double-sided tapes, such as Therm O Web's Mounting Tape, have the sticky adhesive on both sides, so you can join two papers back to back in a firm, tight hold. Scotch Vellum Tape is useful when joining vellum and other thin papers, because there is no show-through. To hold three-dimensional objects, such as micro beads, buttons, or metal charms, try one of the extra-strong scrapbooking tapes available on the market, such as Therm O Web's Super Tape or Suze Weinberg's Wonder Tape. A HERMAfix tape dispenser lets you apply neat double-sided tabs directly to the paper—your fingers don't touch the tape at all. To join large pieces of paper, or to make your own stickers, use double-sided mounting film. Spray adhesives are also convenient for joining large pieces.

Adhesive Dots

Think of adhesive dots as a "dry" form of glue. Instead of dispensing a small glob of liquid glue from a squeeze bottle, you press tiny solid dots of glue or foam onto the paper at the appropriate spots. There's no sticky mess and no wet glue oozing out beyond the edges. A HERMAfix dispenser lets you run a beaded line of glue dots along the paper surface.

Adhesive dots are small—1/4" to 3/8" across—and come in varying thicknesses. A 3-D dot will raise your embellishments up off the surface of the card. For joining sheer or very fine papers or fibers, such as mesh, lace, or tissue paper, Therm O Web's Sticky Dots are ideal. When you lay down this weblike adhesive sheet and join the paper layers together, the dots practically disappear.

Glues

Liquid and gel glues have superior hold, but they can be messy to use. Brush the glue on the wrong side of the paper in a thin, even coat, going out beyond the edges. You can use a chip brush or any flat artist's brush. Each glue product behaves slightly differently. For some people, the tactile activity of brushing glue onto the paper is part of the fun of card making. Once the glue is applied, align the paper glue side down on your project, press into place, and rub firmly to adhere. Wipe off any excess oozing glue promptly and clean your hands frequently to keep your work neat.

If archival longevity is important to you, choose a pH neutral bookbinding or scrapbooking glue. You'll need a strong tacky glue to affix plastic gemstones and similar objects to your paper cards.

MAKING THE CARDS

Each of the card projects in this book includes a materials list and step-by-step instructions. Begin each project by gathering the items you will need, including the tools listed at right. Cut the papers to the specified sizes (see "Cutting Paper" on page 6) so that they are ready to assemble into a card. The paper dimensions follow a width-by-length format, as the paper appears in the card. For example, if the materials list calls for a 1" x 4" piece of red paper, you know that this piece will appear as a vertical strip on the card. Make sure you have all the required adhesives and tools and read through the project instructions and any manufacturer instructions to make sure you understand when and how to use them.

Stickers, rubber stamping, and other embellishments give each card a signature touch. Designers often use particular products that become important to the look of a card. Each project's materials list includes specific manufacturer product information whenever possible to help you to re-create the project card as it is pictured. Of course, you can also venture out on your own and make substitutions. Part of the fun of collage work is working with various media and coming up with new combinations.

BASIC CARD-MAKING TOOLS

These are the tools you will need for every card project.

For measuring and marking:
- Pencil
- Eraser
- Thin, clear plastic grid ruler
- Pencil sharpener

For cutting:
- X-Acto knife or rotary cutter
- Thick, clear plastic grid ruler
- Cutting mat
- Scissors

For folding:
- Bone folder
- Thick, clear acrylic grid ruler

MARK

CHRIS

HELP US RING IN
THE NEW YEAR !
DECEMBER 31, 2004
263 DUPONT STREET
8 O'CLOCK TILL ?

R S V P
515 836 5645

NEW YEAR'S EVE PARTY INVITATION ❧

By Janet Pensiero

Materials

- 8½" x 11" piece of white vellum with iridescent glitter (Grafix)
- 3" x 5" piece of white vellum with iridescent glitter (Grafix)
- 3⅝" x 8½" piece of blue vellum (Grafix)
- 4" x 8½" piece of gray cardstock
- 3" x 7" piece of matte silver cardstock
- 2" x 2" square metal-rimmed vellum tag (Making Memories)
- Two 1" x 1" square metal-rimmed vellum tags (Making Memories)
- Computer and color inkjet printer
- 1 yard of silver organza ribbon, 5/16"-wide (The Card Connection)
- 6 clear glass silver-lined 5 mm beads
- 4 large silver star sequins
- 5 small silver star sequins
- Acid-free double-sided mounting film (Grafix)
- Double-sided vellum tape (3M: Scotch Vellum Tape)
- Fabric glue (Beacon FabriTac)
- Basic card-making tools (see page 11)
- 5 mm star punch
- Template plastic

Encourage guest partici-pation with this festive holiday invitation. Vellum drink tags with each guest's name are attached to the card, ready to bring to the party. Beads and sequins glued to the vellum "champagne" promise an effervescent evening!

Instructions

1. Center the blue vellum on the gray cardstock, aligning the top and bottom edges. Adhere with a 1½" piece of vellum tape centered along the top edge.

2. Trace the champagne and champagne glass patterns (page 15) onto template plastic. Cut out both templates. Trace around the templates with a pencil to mark 1 "champagne" on white vellum and 1 champagne glass on matte silver cardstock. Apply pieces of mounting film to the cardstock, as indicated on the pattern, letting the film extend beyond the marked outline. Cut out both pieces. (See "Templates" on page 6.)

3. Peel off the mounting film's paper backing at the top of the champagne glass only. (The glass base will be adhered in step 8.) Mount the champagne glass on the blue vellum, letting the glass extend ¼" beyond the top edge of the card.

4. Place the vellum "champagne" on the champagne glass and hold the layers together. Punch two star-shaped holes, centered ⁵/₈" from the top edge of the glass and ⁵/₈" apart, through all four layers. Set aside.

5. Compose your party invitation on the computer, sizing the text to fit within a 1¼" x 1" print area. Also type out each guest's name. Print your file in blue ink on white vellum. (See "Working with Text" on page 8, the project photo on page 12, and "Pick a Font" below.)

 PICK A FONT
COPPERPLATE GOTHIC LIGHT

  16-point: guest's names

  11-point: greeting

  8-point: date, time, place, RSVP

6. Apply double-sided mounting film to the back of the printed text. Cut out the invitation and both names a scant ¹/₈" beyond the printed text. Peel off the backing and adhere the invitation to the 2" x 2" tag, allowing a ¹/₂" text-free margin at the top. Adhere each name at an angle to the top left corner of a 1" x 1" tag. Glue a large star sequin to each tag, using fabric glue.

7. Cut three 12" lengths of organza ribbon. Slip a 1" x 1" tag onto one ribbon, drawing through until the ribbon ends are even. Tie a loose overhand knot close to the tag. Run one ribbon tail through a star-shaped hole made in step 4. Tie both tails in a loose overhand knot on the back of the card. Attach the second drink tag to the card in the same way. Trim the ribbon ends at an angle.

8. Fold the third piece of ribbon in half. Insert the looped end through the large tag hole, back to front, and draw through for about 3". Wrap the loop around the stem of the champagne glass and gently draw it close, as shown in the project photograph. Peel off the paper backing and adhere the glass base to the card. Adhere the ribbon to the card under the tag, using a short piece of double-sided tape. Trim the ribbon tails at an angle.

9. Glue a large star sequin to the card front to hold down the bottom point of the champagne. Glue small stars and clear beads to the champagne for effervescence.

DESIGNER'S TIP

Make a custom envelope out of vellum using an opened-out #10 envelope as a template. Create computer-printed text on vellum to address and decorate the envelope.

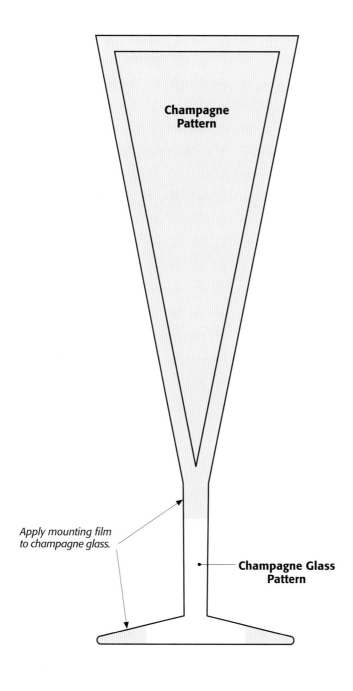

Champagne Pattern

Apply mounting film to champagne glass.

Champagne Glass Pattern

VALENTINE'S DAY CARDS ❦

By Dave Brethauer

Materials (for dangling heart card)

- 8½" x 5⅝" piece of wasabi green cardstock (Memory Box)
- 1¾" x 2¼" piece of pink cardstock, cut with a deckle edger (Memory Box)
- 2" x 2" piece of pink cardstock (Memory Box)
- Floral heart rubber stamp (Savvy Stamps: #149E)
- White pigment inkpad
- White embossing powder
- 5" length of white silk ribbon, 5/16"-wide (May Arts)
- Micro glass beads (Judi-Kins)
- Acid-free double-sided tape (Therm O Web: Mounting Tape)
- Double-sided extra-strong adhesive tape (Therm O Web: Super Tape)
- Tacky glue (api Crafter's Pick: The Ultimate!)
- Basic card-making tools (see page 11)
- Heat tool
- Small scissors

Say "I love you" with whimsical heart shapes to stamp, emboss, or bend from wire. The wire hearts are hammered into paper to create the unique colored interiors. Use this technique with a stamped paper to produce a clever see-through effect.

Instructions (for dangling heart card)

1. Score and fold the wasabi green cardstock in half to make a 4¼" x 5⅝" card, folded edge at left. (See "Folding Paper" on page 5.)

2. Press the deckle-cut edges of the 1¾" x 2¼" pink cardstock into the white inkpad. Sprinkle white embossing powder over the wet ink. Shake off and conserve the excess powder. Heat with a heat tool to melt the powder and emboss the surface. (See "Embossing" on page 7.)

3. Cut a strip of double-sided extra-strong tape, 1/16" wide and 3/4" long. Affix the strip to the pink deckle-edge rectangle, ½" from a short edge and parallel to and centered between the two longer edges, as shown at right. Apply micro glass beads to the surface, pressing to adhere. Shake off and conserve the excess.

4. Stamp a heart in white ink on the 2" x 2" pink cardstock. Emboss as in step 2. Allow to cool. Cut out the heart using small scissors.

5. Tie the white ribbon into a 1¼"-wide bow. Glue the bow to the pink deckle-edge rectangle at the top of the bead chain. Trim the ribbon tails at an angle. Glue the heart from step 4 at the lower end of the bead chain.

6. Mount the heart label on the card front with double-sided tape, allowing a 7/8" margin at the top and a 1¼" margin at each side.

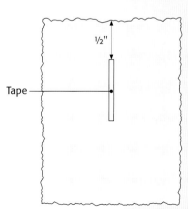

½"

Tape

Materials (for linked hearts card)

- 10" x 3¼" piece of off-white linen cardstock
- 3¾" x 2⅛" piece of chocolate brown cardstock (Memory Box)
- 2" x 4" piece of chocolate brown cardstock (Memory Box)
- 3⅝" x 2" piece of pink cardstock
- Scrap cardstock, at least 2" x 4"
- 20-gauge silver spool wire
- Acid-free double-sided tape (Therm O Web: Mounting Tape)
- Tacky glue (api Crafter's Pick: The Ultimate!)
- Basic card-making tools (see page 11)
- Hammer
- Jewelry pliers
- Cement floor or steel bench block (Rio Grande)
- Wire cutter

Instructions (for linked hearts card)

1. Score and fold the off-white linen cardstock in half to make a 5" x 3¼" card, folded edge at left. (See "Folding Paper" on page 5.)

2. Bend the silver wire with pliers into a heart shape, to match pattern A on page 19. Clip the wire heart free from the spool. Make a second wire heart to match pattern B. Make a looped piece to match pattern C.

3. Layer the 2" x 4" chocolate brown cardstock and the scrap cardstock on a cement floor or steel bench block. Lay wire heart A on one end of the brown cardstock. Tap with a hammer until the wire cuts through the brown cardstock only. Repeat with wire heart B. Hammer wire piece C flat, without any cardstock backing.

4. Lay hearts A and B on the pink cardstock. Place piece C in between, letting the hearts overlap it slightly at each end, as indicated on the pattern. Allow at least a ¼" margin all around, as shown in the project photo (above). Secure the wire pieces with tacky glue.

5. Center and mount the pink cardstock on the 3¾" x 2⅛" chocolate brown cardstock, using double-sided tape. Center and mount the layered piece on the card front.

Materials (for overlapping hearts card)

- 5" x 10" piece of off-white linen cardstock
- 3" x 4" piece of natural cardstock
- 3" x 4" piece of pink cardstock
- 2¼" x 3⁷⁄₁₆" piece of chocolate brown cardstock (Memory Box)
- Script heart rubber stamp (PSX: Heart in Love #F2841)
- Brown pigment inkpad (VersaColor: Pinecone)
- 20-gauge silver spool wire
- Acid-free double-sided tape (Therm O Web: Mounting Tape)
- Tacky glue (api Crafter's Pick: The Ultimate!)
- Basic card-making tools (see page 11)
- Hammer
- Jewelry pliers
- Cement floor or steel bench block (Rio Grande)
- Wire cutter

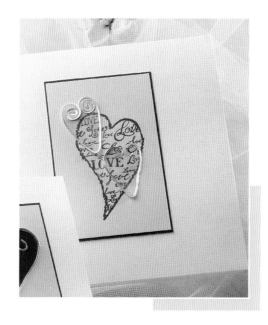

Instructions (for overlapping hearts card)

1. Score and fold the off-white linen cardstock in half, to make a 5" x 5" card, folded edge at top. (See "Folding Paper" on page 5.)

2. Using brown ink, stamp one heart on pink cardstock and one heart on natural cardstock.

3. Bend the silver wire with pliers into a heart shape, to match pattern D (below left). Clip the wire heart free from the spool. Make a second wire heart to match pattern E. Clip free.

4. Lay the stamped pink cardstock right side up on a cement floor or steel bench block. Lay wire heart D on the cardstock, overlapping the stamped heart so that the top left area of the stamped heart is visible in the bottom area of the wire heart. Tap with a hammer until the wire cuts through the cardstock. Repeat the process with heart E, placing it to overlap the lower right of the stamped heart.

5. Place hearts D and E on the natural cardstock, aligning the stamped areas. Adhere with tacky glue. Trim the natural cardstock to 2⅛" x 3⅜", allowing at least a ¼" margin beyond the hearts all around.

6. Center and mount the natural cardstock on the chocolate brown cardstock, using double-sided tape. Center and mount the layered piece on the card front.

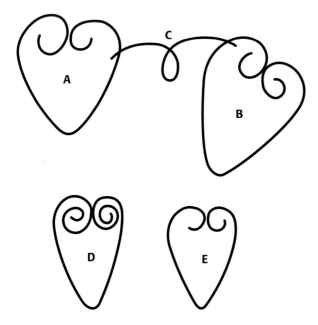

I D O

PRESS

Press as You Sew. Press all seams open unless otherwise indicated, clipping where necessary so seams will lay flat.

Press pleats and straight seams on **Flat Surface.**

Press darts and curved seams over **Rounded Surface.**

B R I D E

BRIDAL SHOWER INVITATIONS ❧

By Saralyn Ewald,
Creative Coordinator for
Archiver's—The Photo
Memory Store

Materials (for paper doll dress card)

- 8½" x 11" piece of white cardstock
- 8½" x 5½" piece of pale pink cardstock
- 5" x 6¼" piece of a vintage dress pattern instruction sheet
- ³/8" pink paper flower (EK Success Jolee's By You)
- Yellow typewriter alphabet stickers (Nostalgiques by Rebecca Sower: Aged Typewriter)
- Two ³/8" x 1¼" brass hinges
- Four ⅛" silver eyelets (Making Memories)
- 8" length of pink embroidered satin ribbon, 5/16"-wide
- Silver glitter glue (PSX: Diamond Sparkles)
- Double-sided dry tacky tape (Suze Weinberg: Wonder Tape)
- pH neutral PVA bookbinding glue (Books By Hand)
- Black fine-point permanent pen
- Basic card-making tools (see page 11)
- Eyelet setter (Making Memories)
- Chip brush or flat artist's brush
- Hammer
- Metal ruler
- Perforating blade (EK Success: Cutter Bee Bugs Perforator)
- Small scissors

Simultaneously feminine and funky, these shower invitations are perfect for the modern bride. Adorn one card with pearly white buttons, glue-on gloves, and a not-to-be-missed diamond engagement ring. For the working girl, try old-fashioned typewriter key stickers, a paper doll dress cutout, and the instruction sheet from an old dress pattern.

Instructions (for paper doll dress card)

1. Score and fold the pink cardstock in half to make a 4¼" x 5½" card, folded edge at the left. (See "Folding Paper" on page 5.)

2. Brush bookbinding glue on the card front. Center and mount the vintage pattern instructions on the card front, pressing to adhere. Fold the excess paper at the left edge onto the back of the card and glue down. Trim off the excess even with the edges of the card. Allow to dry.

3. Cut 2 parallel perforated lines on the card front, ½" and 1⅛" from the fold, by drawing a perforating blade against a metal ruler.

4. Run pink ribbon between the perforated lines. Secure the ribbon ends on the inside of the card with dabs of bookbinding glue.

5. Photocopy the paper doll dress (page 22) onto white cardstock. Cut out the dress, including the tabs, along the outside edge of the black outline, using small scissors. Save the scraps.

6. Apply glitter glue to the dress sash. Apply dots of glitter glue along the hem. Glue a ³/₈" paper flower to the dress for a corsage.

7. Cut a few narrow strips from the white cardstock scraps and glue them to the back of the dress cutout. Glue the dress to the card front, ¹/₈" to the right of the ribbon and 1" below the top edge. The strips will raise the dress up off the surface, for a 3-D look.

8. Apply typewriter alphabet stickers across the bottom of the card, about ¹/₈" above the edge, to spell out *BRIDE*. Let the *E* sticker hang off the right edge. Place the *B* sticker ¹/₄" to the right of the ribbon. Place the remaining three stickers evenly spaced in between. Trim the *E* sticker even with the edge of the card.

9. Set silver eyelets in the holes of the small brass hinges. Attach the hinges to the front and back of the card with double-sided tape.

Materials (for engagement ring card)

- 4³/₄" x 9¹/₂" piece of white cold press watercolor paper (Strathmore)
- 5" x 5" piece of white cold press watercolor paper (Strathmore)
- Scraps of white cold press watercolor paper (Strathmore)
- 4¹/₄" x 4¹/₄" piece of pink pearlescent paper
- 3" x 3" piece of crackle pattern paper with torn edges (Creative Imaginations: Debbie Mumm)
- Scraps of white cardstock
- Pair of 1⁵/₈" bridal glove cutouts (EK Success: Jolee's By You)
- Wooden tile alphabet stickers (Making Memories)
- Engagement ring rubber stamp (Toomuchfun Rubberstamps)
- Dark brown dye-based inkpad (Clearsnap Inc.: Ancient Page Dye Ink in Chocolate)
- ³/₄" open gold oval (Scrap Works: Conchos)
- 4" length of thin white string
- 24 assorted small white and ivory buttons
- Silver glitter glue (PSX: Diamond Sparkles)
- Double-sided dry tacky tape (Suze Weinberg: Wonder Tape)
- 3-D glue dot (Glue Dots International: Pop Up Glue Dots)
- pH neutral PVA bookbinding glue (Books By Hand)
- Basic card-making tools (see page 11)
- ¹/₈" hole punch
- ⁹/₁₆" flower punch (EK Success: Paper Shapers Pom-Pom)
- Flat artist's brush
- Metal ruler

Instructions (for engagement ring card)

1. Score and fold the 4³/₄" x 9¹/₂" piece of watercolor paper in half to make a 4³/₄" x 4³/₄" card, folded edge at top. (See "Folding Paper" on page 5.)

2. Brush bookbinding glue on the wrong side of the pink pearlescent paper. Center and mount the paper on the card front. Allow to dry.

3. Brush bookbinding glue on the wrong side of the crackle pattern paper. Center and mount the paper on the 5" x 5" watercolor paper. Allow to dry, preferably overnight.

4. Lightly mark a 2¹/₂" x 2¹/₂" square in the center of the 5" x 5" watercolor paper by measuring in 1¹/₄" from each edge. Cut out the interior square using a ruler and X-Acto knife. The crackle pattern paper will frame the opening.

5. Punch the gold oval through the paper at the top center of the frame, about ¹/₂" below the top edge. Bend back the prongs on the reverse side to hold it in place. Punch three flowers from a scrap of watercolor paper and glue them to the frame at random, using bookbinding glue. Attach buttons around the top half of the frame opening and up around the gold oval, using small pieces of double-sided tape.

6. Cut a few strips from the white cardstock scraps. Glue the strips to the back of the frame, using bookbinding glue. Center and mount the frame on the card front, using bookbinding glue. The strips will raise the frame up off the surface, for a 3-D look.

7. Apply alphabet tile stickers to the lower right corner of the pink framed opening to spell *I DO*. Mount the gloves in the middle with double-sided tape, overlapping the hands as shown in the project photograph. Apply a band of glitter glue above each cuff.

8. Stamp an engagement ring in dark brown ink on a scrap of white watercolor paper. Apply glitter glue to the stone area. Allow to dry. Cut out the stamped image, making a ⁵/₈" x ⁷/₈" rectangle. Cut the rectangle diagonally across two corners to make a tag shape. Punch a hole at the tapered end, using a ¹/₈" hole punch.

9. Thread thin string through the tag hole and tie a knot. Loop the other end of the string around the ring finger of the left-hand glove, allowing about 1³/₄" of string in between. Secure the string on the wrong side of the glove with double-sided tape and cut off the excess. Mount the ring tag on left edge of the frame with a 3-D glue dot.

You're Invited

to an Easter Egg Hunt

Happy Easter

EASTER CARD
AND INVITATION 🌿

By Dawn Anderson

Materials (for Easter baby card)

- 8½" x 11" piece of medium blue-green fiber paper
- 9¼" x 6³/8" piece of flecked yellow paper with torn edge on one 6³/8" side
- 5" x 6³/8" piece of yellow mottled paper
- 5" x 6³/8" piece of yellow speckled mulberry paper
- 2½" x 3¼" piece of medium blue-green vellum
- 2" x 2⁷/8" Easter photo (see "Designer's Tip" on page 26)
- Computer and color inkjet printer
- ¼" yard of baby blue silk ribbon, ¼"-wide
- 7⁵/8" length of blue-and-green picot-edge trim (Mokuba)
- Blue-green letter *E* stone (Creative Imaginations: Sharon Soneff: Poemstone)
- Acid-free double-sided tape (Therm O Web: Mounting Tape)
- Adhesive dots sheet (Therm O Web: Sticky Dots)
- Tacky glue (api Crafter's Pick: The Ultimate!)
- Basic card-making tools (see page 11)

Fine-quality sepia-tone images are possible on a photocopier—if you know a few tricks. Combine your photocopying skills, beautiful art papers, and a few carefully selected trims to create these Easter card masterpieces.

Instructions (for Easter baby card)

1. Tear the 5" x 6³/8" piece of yellow mulberry paper diagonally into two pieces, starting at the upper right corner and ending 1" above the lower left corner. Mount the lower right torn-off portion on the yellow mottled paper, right and lower edges aligned, using an adhesive dots sheet.

2. Using a computer, type *Happy aster*, allowing a 1¹/8" margin at the left side and a 1³/4" margin at the top. Leave a 1" space for the *E* stone, to be inserted later. To match the project card, use the Bookman Old Style font in a 44-point size. (See "Working with Text" on page 8.)

3. Print the file on medium blue-green fiber paper. Select gray (not black) as the printing color for a better match to the silver *E* on the stone. Trim the printed greeting to 6³/8" x 3¼", centering the greeting 1" above the lower edge.

Materials (for bunny invitation)

- 8½" x 11" piece of cream cardstock
- 8½" x 11" piece of yellow ribbed cardstock
- 8½" x 11" piece of blue speckled paper (Carolee's Creations Blue Dust)
- 6¼" x 7¼" piece of yellow mottled cardstock with torn edge on one 6¼" side
- ¼" x 8½" piece of medium blue-green fiber paper
- Copyright-free bunny image (Dover Publications *Treasury of Animal Illustrations: From Eighteenth-Century Sources*)
- White pigment inkpad (Color Box "Frost White")
- Yellow speckled embossing powder (Stamp'n Around: EP147 Eggnog)
- Turquoise textured embossing powder (Stamp'n Around: EP211 Turquoise Tex)
- Lilac textured embossing powder (Stamp'n Around: EP209 Lilac Tex)
- Clear ultra-thick embossing enamel (Ranger Industries: Suze Weinberg)
- Computer and printer
- Photocopier service, such as Kinko's
- 6" length of green textured thread (On the Surface Embellishments: It's a Boy IBT135)
- 3 blank oval page pebbles (Making Memories)
- Acid-free double-sided tape (Therm O Web: Mounting Tape)
- Paper-thin adhesive dots (Therm O Web: Memory Zots)
- Tacky glue (api Crafter's Pick: The Ultimate!)
- Basic card-making tools (see page 11)
- Heat tool

4. Mount the greeting on the yellow flecked paper with double-sided tape, overhanging the right edge by ¼" as shown. Mount the overhanging edge to the left edge of the layered papers from step 1.

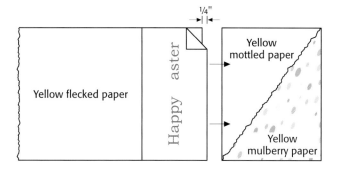

5. Score and fold the card in half so that the torn edge extends beyond the right edge of the card. (See "Folding Paper" on page 5.)

6. Cut the blue ribbon into four equal pieces. Place each ribbon diagonally across a corner of the photo. Fold the ends to the back of the photo and secure with double-sided tape.

7. Center and mount the photo on blue-green vellum using double-sided tape. Center and mount the vellum on the layered yellow papers, partially covering the diagonal tear line.

8. Glue the blue-and-green trim over the join between the yellow and blue-green papers, using tacky glue. Fold and glue the ends to the inside front cover. Adhere the letter *E* stone to the open space to complete the greeting.

Instructions (for bunny invitation)

1. Set a color photocopier for sepia-tone printing. Photocopy the copyright-free bunny image onto cream cardstock, sizing the bunny to about $3^{3}/_{4}$" long and $2^{5}/_{8}$" high. Trim the cardstock to $4^{3}/_{8}$" x $3^{1}/_{4}$", making a torn lower edge.

 DESIGNER'S TIP

Before making a photocopy, use a liquid correction pen to white out areas of the image that you don't want to use. You can easily eliminate unwanted captions, background figures, and other details that would be distracting on your card.

2. Run green textured thread across the bottom of the bunny illustration, about $^{3}/_{8}$" from the torn edge. Fold the thread ends to the back side. Secure with double-sided tape. Set aside.

3. Using a computer, type and center the words *You're Invited* $2^{5}/_{8}$" down from the top of the page. Scroll down $4^{7}/_{8}$". Type and center *to an Easter* and *Hunt*, allowing a $1^{1}/_{16}$" space between *Easter* and *Hunt*. To match the project card, use the Lucida Calligraphy font in a 22-point size, changing to 14-point for the words *to an*. Create a second file and type the word *Egg* in 22-point at the top of the page. Print the first file onto yellow ribbed cardstock. Print the second file onto blue speckled paper. (See "Working with Text" on page 8.)

4. Trim the yellow ribbed cardstock to $6^{1}/_{4}$" x $9^{1}/_{4}$", centering the printed message across the width and leaving a $2^{5}/_{8}$" margin at the top.

5. Score and fold the yellow ribbed cardstock 2" from and parallel to the upper edge, to create a 2" flap. (See "Folding Paper" on page 5.) Mount the yellow mottled cardstock on the 2" flap with double-sided tape to form the inside/back of the card. The torn edge of the yellow mottled cardstock should extend beyond the lower edge of the card front.

6. Adhere an oval page pebble at an angle to the printed word *Egg*. Turn the work over and burnish on the back side with a bone folder. Trim away the excess paper even with the pebble edge. Mount the page pebble on the card front between *Easter* and *Hunt*, using tacky glue.

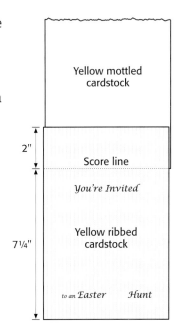

7. From the remaining blue speckled paper, cut a 4" x $4^{3}/_{4}$" rectangle. Center and mount the rectangle on the card front between the two message lines, using double-sided tape. Mount the bunny illustration on the blue speckled paper, $^{3}/_{16}$" from the top and side edges, using double-sided tape.

8. Apply white pigment ink to a page pebble. Immediately sprinkle with yellow speckled embossing enamel. Shake off and conserve the excess powder. Heat with heat tool until the powder melts and diffuses into a smooth surface. Immediately sprinkle more powder onto the surface and heat until melted. Repeat once more with clear ultra thick embossing powder. The resulting page pebble will resemble a yellow speckled egg.

9. Repeat step 8, using the remaining page pebble and the turquoise and lilac embossing powders, to make a blue speckled egg.

10. Remove and discard the adhesive backing from both page pebbles. Glue the pebbles to the right side of the card under the bunny's nose, using tacky glue.

11. Cut two $^{1}/_{8}$" strips from the blue-green fiber paper. Cut in half, wad up in a tight ball, and release to make Easter grass. Secure the grass to the card under the eggs, using adhesive dots.

FLORAL BIRTHDAY AND THANK-YOU CARDS

By Christine Adolph

Materials (for birthday card)

- 11³/₄" x 6¹/₄" piece of white cardstock
- 3¹/₂" x 3¹/₂"* piece of bright pink paper
- 3¹/₈" x 3¹/₈"* piece of hand-writing printed paper (The Card Connection: TCP0604)
- 2³/₄" x 2¹/₄"* piece of gold metallic paper
- 2¹/₄" x 2¹/₄"* piece of blue paper
- 1¹/₄" x 1¹/₄"* piece of pressed flower sheet (The Card Connection: TCP0705)
- Tissue paper dress pattern

- 8¹/₂" x 11" piece of transparency film
- *Happy* turquoise wire word (The Card Connection)
- Sewing thread: magenta, blue, yellow
- Gel glue (Golden: Gel Medium)
- Basic card-making tools (see page 11)
- Chip brush or flat artist's brush
- Pinking shears
- Sewing machine
- Hand-sewing needle

*Approximate size; cut freehand

> The secret to these quirky, artsy cards is to eyeball the cutting dimensions. Use the measurements listed in the materials list as a guide, but cut your collage papers free-hand. As you assemble your collage, retrim the papers to make them fit together any way you like. The resulting look is organic and lively.

Instructions (for birthday card)

1. **Select an interesting section of the tissue paper dress pattern to use for your collage. Cut out a piece from this section about ¹/₂" larger all around than the white cardstock.**

2. **Brush a smooth, even coat of gel glue on one side of the white cardstock. Lay the cut tissue piece on top and smooth it with your fingers. Brush a thin coat of gel glue over the top as a sealer. Allow to dry.**

3. **Score and fold the tissue/cardstock piece in half, tissue on the outside, to make a 5⁷/₈" x 3¹/₈" card, folded edge at left. (See "Folding Paper" on page 5.) Cut along the three outside edges with pinking shears.**

4. **Brush gel glue on the back of the bright pink paper. Center and mount it on the card front. Glue and layer the handwriting printed paper, the gold metallic paper, the blue paper, and the pressed flower piece to the card front, centering each piece on the one under it, except the gold metallic, which fills in the top left corner. Be sure your collage includes a narrow bright pink border. Allow to dry.**

DESIGNER'S TIP

When you are collaging multiple papers, do a dry run before you glue anything down. That way, you can see how the papers will look when layered and make needed trims before things get messy.

5. Photocopy the birthday dictionary text (below) onto transparency film. Cut the film about ¼" beyond the text all around, making a 2¾" x ¾" piece.

bĭrth′dāy

6. Open the card flat. Drop the feed dogs on the sewing machine. Using magenta thread, zigzag around the edges of the pink paper. Using blue thread, zigzag around the edges of the pressed flower piece. Place the printed transparency film on the card below the pressed flower piece. Using yellow thread, sew down the edges in straight stitch.

7. Place the *happy* wire word at an angle above the pressed flowers. Tack down using needle and thread.

Materials (for thank-you card)

- 5¼" x 6¾" piece of lavender cardstock
- ⅝" x 1¾"* piece of blue paper
- ⅝" x 1¾"* piece of pressed flower sheet (The Card Connection: TCP0705)
- 4" x 2½"* piece of bright pink paper
- 2⅜" x 2⅜"* piece of gold metallic paper
- 1½" x ⅝"* piece of handwriting printed paper (The Card Connection: TCP0604)
- Old textbook
- 2" lilac flower appliqué (Flower Patch: Decorative Details)
- Sewing thread: blue, purple
- 3 assorted plastic gemstones, 5/16" across
- Gel glue (Golden: Gel Medium)
- Fabric glue (Beacon: FabriTac)
- Basic card-making tools (see page 11)
- Chip brush or flat artist's brush
- Deckle edge scissors
- Sewing machine

Approximate size; cut freehand

Instructions (for thank-you card)

1. Score and fold the lavender cardstock in half to make a 5¼" x 3⅜" card, folded edge at top. (See "Folding Paper" on page 5.) Cut along the three outside edges with deckle edge scissors.

2. Brush a smooth, even coat of gel glue on the back side of the bright pink paper. Center and glue the paper to the card front, pressing to adhere.

3. Arrange the gold metallic, blue, pressed flower, and handwriting papers on the pink paper, referring to the project photo for placement. Overlap or retrim the paper edges as needed to create a collage with a narrow bright pink border. Glue in place with gel glue. Allow to dry.

4. Open the card flat. Drop the feed dogs on the sewing machine. Using purple thread, zigzag around the edge of the pink paper. Let some of the stitches overlap onto the collaged papers. Using blue thread, sew a loopy design in straight stitch on the blue paper.

5. Glue 3 gemstones to the blue paper, using fabric glue.

6. Select and cut out 6 individual capital letters from the old textbook to spell *THANKS*. Lay out the letters and the lilac flower appliqué on the gold paper, as shown in the project photo. Glue in place, using gel glue.

GRADUATION CARDS 🌿

By Saralyn Ewald
Creative Coordinator
for Archiver's—
The Photo Memory Store

Materials (for square card)

- 3½" x 8" piece of pale green cardstock
- 4¼" x 4¼" piece of kraft-colored cardstock
- One 4¼" x 4¼" and one 2" x 2¾" piece of ivory paper with French black script (7 Gypsies: Large Script)
- 1¾" x 2¼" piece of corrugated paper, ribs parallel to the 1¾" edges (DMD Corrugated "Darks")
- 1½" x 1½" piece of green accounting paper (Ampad: Columnar Pad)
- Two 3¼" x 3⅞" pieces of an old map
- ¾" x 6½" strip of page text from an old book, with one torn edge on a 6½" side
- 4¼" x 6¼" glassine envelope
- ⅞"-diameter metal-rimmed vellum tag (Making Memories)
- 2¼" x 5" piece of gold metallic self-adhesive mesh (Magic Mesh)
- Black uppercase alphabet stickers (Creative Imaginations: Sharon Soneff: Flea Market Blocks)
- Black typewriter alphabet stickers (Nostalgiques by Rebecca Sower: Aged Typewriter)
- 2" alphabet stencils (U.S. Stamp & Sign: 2" Stencil Kit)
- Calligraphic alphabet stencils (Wordsworth: Fancy Caps)
- Printer's uppercase alphabet rubber stamps (Hero Arts)
- Printer's lowercase alphabet rubber stamps (Hero Arts)
- Black dye-based inkpad (Clearsnap, Inc.: Ancient Page Dye Ink in Coal Black)
- Five ⅛" gold eyelets (Making Memories)
- Toy compass, ¾" diameter
- Burgundy chenille flat yarn (On the Surface Embellishments: Victorian Dreams VDT124)
- 9" length of thin hemp cord
- White acrylic paint
- Double-sided dry tacky tape (Suze Weinberg: Wonder Tape)
- pH neutral PVA bookbinding glue (Books By Hand)
- Red colored pencil
- Basic card-making tools (see page 11)
- ⅛" hole punch (Fiskars)
- Artist's brush
- Chip brush or flat artist's brush
- Small stencil brush
- Eyelet setter (Making Memories)
- Hammer

Encourage a new graduate to chart the course ahead. The printed papers and stickers in these card collages include ledgers, journals, maps, typewriter keys, and a measuring tape. There's even some school-ruled paper, for one last nostalgic glance backward before venturing toward that new horizon.

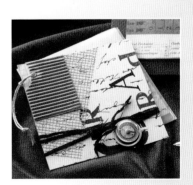

Instructions (for square card)

FRONT TAG

1. Brush bookbinding glue on the back of the 4¼" x 4¼" ivory paper, using a chip brush or flat artist's brush. Mount the ivory paper on the kraft-colored cardstock. Allow to dry.

2. Rotate the tag so that the script writing is upside-down. Choose from the assorted stencils, stamps, and stickers to print the word *Grad* up the right edge of the tag. To match the project shown, stencil a 2" *G* with black paint, using a small stencil brush; stamp two uppercase *R*'s in black ink, letting one letter run off the edge of the card; apply a black uppercase *A* sticker; and stamp a lowercase *d* in black ink, letting it run off the edge of the card.

3. Apply gold metallic self-adhesive mesh across the left side of the tag at an angle. Trim off the overhanging mesh even with the tag edges.

4. Brush bookbinding glue on the back of the green accounting paper. Mount the paper on the top left corner of the tag.

5. Using small scissors, make a curved cut across the top left corner of the corrugated paper. Brush bookbinding glue on the back of the corrugated paper. Mount the paper on the top left corner of the tag, straight edges aligned, so that the green paper peeks through the cutaway area.

6. Wrap the burgundy yarn three times around the tag, 1" above the lower edge. Tie the ends together, slip the metal-rimmed vellum tag onto the yarn, and complete the knot. Mount the toy compass on the metal-rimmed tag using double-sided tape.

ENVELOPE AND CARD

1. Score and fold the pale green cardstock in half to make a 3¼" x 4" card, folded edge at top. (See "Folding Paper" on page 5.)

2. Brush bookbinding glue on the reverse side of each map. Mount the maps on the inside of the card, side edges aligned. Keep the middle fold line clear.

3. Brush white paint over the maps, using an artist's brush, to create a washed-out look. Allow to dry.

4. Tear the 2" x 2¾" piece of ivory paper diagonally in half. Brush bookbinding glue on the reverse side of both pieces. Mount one piece on the lower right corner of the card front, aligning the corner edges. Mount the other piece on the inside of the card, also at the lower right corner.

5. Brush bookbinding glue on the reverse side of the book text strip. Mount the strip on the inside of the card, starting at the top left corner and aligning it along the left edge.

6. Use the calligraphic stencils to trace the letters *G* and *O* on the top inside page of the card. Color selected areas of the lettering with a red pencil.

7. Stamp *go in the direction of your dreams* in black ink on the bottom inside page, using the lowercase alphabet stamps. Apply typewriter alphabet stickers *N*, *S*, *E*, and *W* evenly spaced across the bottom of the same page.

8. Cut off one end of the glassine envelope to make a 4¼" x 4¼" packet with an open top edge. Starting at the top left corner, measure ½" to the right and ⅝" down. Punch a hole, using a ⅛" hole punch. Punch three more holes, 1" apart, along the left edge, ending ⅝" from the bottom edge. Set a gold eyelet into each hole, using an eyelet setter and a hammer. (See "Installing Eyelets" on page 9.) Slip the folded card inside the envelope.

FINAL ASSEMBLY

Hold the tag and glassine envelope together, top left corners aligned. Use a pencil to mark the glassine eyelet position on the tag. Punch a corresponding 1/8" hole in the tag. Set with a gold eyelet. Hitch the tag and glassine envelope together with hemp cord.

Materials (for rectangular card)

- 7 1/2" x 6" piece of red textured paper
- 2 5/8" x 5" piece of kraft-colored paper (Carolee's Creations: Tan Hues)
- 2 5/8" x 4" piece of reproduction antique map with torn edge on one 2 5/8" side
- 2 1/8" x 1 3/8" piece of brick red cardstock
- 1 1/4" x 6 1/2" piece of school-ruled paper (Carolee's Creations: School Work)
- 2 5/8" x 5" kraft-colored tag (Archiver's)
- 2 5/8" x 5/8" piece of ruler sticker (Nostalgiques by Rebecca Sower: Rule of Thumb)
- Antique uppercase wooden type
- Black dye-based inkpad (Clearsnap Inc.: Ancient Page Dye Ink in Coal Black)
- Round pewter alphabet charms (Making Memories)
- Plain-notched pewter photo corners (Making Memories)
- Double-sided dry tacky tape (Suze Weinberg: Wonder Tape)
- 3-D foam adhesive dots (All Night Media: Pop Dots)
- Basic card-making tools (see page 11)
- 1/4" hole punch
- 1/8" "anywhere" hole punch (Making Memories)

Instructions (for rectangular card)

1. Score and fold the red paper in half to make a 3 3/4" x 6" card, folded edge at left. (See "Folding Paper" on page 5.)

2. On the inside of the card front, draft a light pencil line parallel to and 1/2" from the fold. Punch four holes on this line, 5/8" from the top edge and spaced 5/8" apart, using a 1/8" "anywhere" hole punch. Erase the pencil line.

3. Write some words in pencil on the school-ruled paper. Erase the words to give the paper a used look. Mount the paper on the right edge of the card front, angled slightly toward the top right corner, using double-sided tape. Trim off the excess even with edges of the card.

4. Stamp uppercase letters in black ink across the school-ruled paper and partially onto the card.

5. Mount the kraft-colored paper on the tag, using double-sided tape. Punch a hole in the paper to match the tag hole, using a 1/4" punch.

6. Mount the map on the tag, torn edge near the hole, using double-sided tape. Apply the ruler sticker across the tag, parallel to and 7/8" from the bottom edge.

7. Mount uppercase and lowercase pewter charms on the brick red cardstock, centered in two rows, to spell out *GoOd LUck*, using small pieces of double-sided tape. Mount the cardstock on the tag directly above the ruler sticker, with right edges aligned, using double-sided tape.

8. Mount the tag to the card front, roughly centered, using foam adhesive dots to raise it off the surface. Mount the pewter corners on the top and bottom right corners, using double-sided tape.

FRIENDSHIP GREETING CARDS 🌿

*By Sonya Anderson
Instructor for Archiver's—
The Photo Memory Store*

Materials (for rectangular card)

- 7" x 7½" piece of pink cardstock
- 6⅞" x 7⅜" piece of light pink textured cardstock
- 1⅜" x 1⅜" square of black suede paper (SEI Industries)
- Scrap of brown diamond-textured handmade paper (Creative Papers Online)
- 2½" x 7" piece of black-and-white checked fabric (Waverly)
- 2¼" x 2¼" pewter frame with 1⅜" x 1⅜" opening (Making Memories)
- 1⁹⁄₁₆" x 1¾" Euripides eyelet quote (Making Memories)
- ⅛" pewter heart snap (Making Memories)
- ½ yard of burgundy ribbon, ⅜" wide (May Arts)
- Black sewing thread
- One ⅞" black button (Making Memories)

- Three ⁹⁄₁₆" black buttons (Making Memories)
- Double-sided photo tape (3L)
- Double-sided dry tacky tape (Suze Weinberg: Wonder Tape)
- pH neutral scrapbook glue (Magic Scraps: Scrappy Glue)
- Basic card-making tools (see page 11)
- 1½" x 1½" square punch
- 1" x 1" square punch
- ⅛" "anywhere" hole punch (Making Memories)
- Chip brush or flat artist's brush
- Eyelet setter (Making Memories)
- Hammer
- Hand-sewing needle
- Paper piercer
- Sewing machine

Design a collage using everything that makes you happy: eyelet quotes, buttons, pewter hearts, bits of ribbon, a friendship rubber stamp. Then give your collage creation to a friend and make her happy too!

Instructions (for rectangular card)

1. Score and fold the pink cardstock in half to make a 3½" x 7" card, folded edge at left. Score and fold the light pink cardstock in half to make the slightly smaller card liner. (See "Folding Paper" on page 5.)

2. Fold the fabric strip around the folded edge of the card, to create a 1½"-wide spine on card front and a 1"-wide spine on card back. Adhere with double-sided photo tape.

Nothing can
come between
true friends
- Euripides

A friend
is one who knows
all about you and
likes you
anyway

FRIEND

3. Cut the square of black suede paper diagonally in half. Align and mount the triangles on the top right and bottom right corners of the card front using double-sided photo tape.

4. Open the card flat. Using a long stitch length and black thread, machine stitch the card front ¼" from the outside edges and the fold line all around.

5. Cut the ribbon in half. Align and mount each ribbon over a raw edge of the fabric spine, using double-sided photo tape. Fold the ribbon ends onto the reverse side of the card and adhere.

6. Use the punches to cut a 1½" x 1½" square and a 1" x 1" square from the brown handmade paper. Hand-sew a ⅞" button to the larger square, using a needle and black thread. Punch a hole in the middle of the smaller square, using a ⅛" hole punch. Install a heart snap, using an eyelet setter and a hammer. (See "Installing Eyelets" on page 9.)

7. Place both squares on the card front at an angle, the larger square near the top and the smaller near the bottom, as shown in the project photo (page 36). Brush scrapbook glue on the back of each square, using a chip brush or flat artist's brush, and press to adhere. Glue the pewter frame to the card around the larger square.

8. Punch a hole in the card front, ⅞" from the right edge and 2½" from the bottom edge, using the ⅛" hole punch. Install the Euripides eyelet, using an eyelet setter and a hammer. (See "Installing Eyelets" on page 9.)

9. Glue the three smaller buttons in a column to the card front's lower spine, spacing them about ½" apart and ⅜" from the lower edge, using scrapbook glue. Allow to dry. Pierce the card front through each button hole, using a paper piercer. Hand-sew each button to the card, using a needle and black thread.

10. Slip the card liner from step 1 inside the card, align the folds, and adhere with double-sided tacky tape.

Materials (for square card)

- 5" x 10" piece of purple cardstock
- 4" x 4¼" piece of ivory cardstock with four torn edges
- 3" x 4" piece of purple mottled handmade paper (Creative Papers Online)
- ¾" x 3⅛" piece of purple striped paper with one long edge torn (Keeping Memories Alive)
- Friendship quotes block rubber stamp (PSX: K-3220)
- Woodblock alphabet rubber stamps (Hero Arts)
- Black dye-based inkpad (Tsukineko: Brilliance Ink)
- Pewter friendship eyelet plaque (Making Memories)
- Pewter heart eyelet shape (Making Memories)
- Pewter mesh heart eyelet shape (Making Memories)
- 12" length each of 2 novelty yarns (Making Memories: Funky Fibers)
- Ivory sewing thread
- Double-sided photo tape (3L)
- Basic card-making tools (see page 11)
- ⅛" hole punch
- Eyelet setter
- Hammer
- Iron
- Sewing machine
- Template plastic

Instructions (for square card)

1. Score and fold the purple cardstock in half to make a 5" x 5" card, folded edge at top. (See "Folding Paper" on page 5.)

2. Center and stamp the friendship quotes block in black ink on the ivory cardstock. Allow to dry.

3. Wrinkle the ivory cardstock, and then iron it flat. Mount the ivory cardstock on the card front, as close to the upper right corner as possible but still letting some purple show through, using a few pieces of double-sided tape.

4. Open the card flat. Using ivory thread and a long stitch length, machine stitch the ivory cardstock to the card in four straight lines, each about 1/4" beyond the stamped image.

5. Close the card. Use double-sided vellum tape to mount the striped paper on the upper left corner of the card. Orient the torn edge toward the stitched piece.

6. Trace the heart pattern (below) onto template plastic. Cut out the template. Trace around the template with a pencil to mark 1 heart on purple handmade paper. Cut out the heart. (See "Templates" on page 6.)

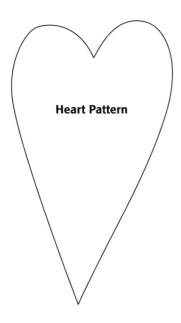

Heart Pattern

7. Mount the heart on the lower left side of the card with double-sided photo tape, partially covering the other pieces.

8. Punch a hole in the card front, 2" from right edge and 2" from top edge, using a 1/8" hole punch. Install the pewter friendship eyelet plaque, using an eyelet setter and a hammer. In the same way, install a pewter heart eyelet shape 1 3/8" from left edge and 1" from bottom edge. Install a pewter mesh heart shape 5/8" from right edge and 1/8" from top edge. (See "Installing Eyelets" on page 9.)

9. Stamp the word *FRIEND* in black ink across the bottom of the card, using the alphabet rubber stamps. Angle the letters and space them about 1/8" apart for a playful look.

10. Wrap the novelty yarns around the card front, tie the ends in a knot, and cut off the excess.

WEDDING
INVITATIONS ❦

*By Saralyn Ewald
Creative Coordinator for
Archiver's—The Photo
Memory Store*

Materials (for wings invitation)

- 8½" x 11" piece of white cardstock
- 8" x 5⅛" piece of light blue cardstock
- 8½" x 11" piece of vellum
- 3½" x 1½" piece of sheet music paper, with torn left and bottom edges (Sandylion: Heritage Paper Music)
- 1¾" x 1½" piece of sheet music paper, with four torn edges (Sandylion: Heritage Paper Music)
- 2" x 2" piece of blue floral print paper (Anna Griffin: #AG020)
- 1" x 1⅛" piece of mat board
- 1" x 1⅛" color photocopy of a black-and-white portrait
- Clip art wings (Dover Publications *Early Advertising Alphabets, Initials & Typographic Ornaments*)
- Photocopier service, such as Kinko's
- Dove rubber stamp (PSX B-3440)
- Gold pigment inkpad (Tsukineko Inc.: Encore Ultimate Metallic)
- Gold embossing powder (Ranger Industries)

- Jet black inkpad for nonporous surfaces (Tsukineko Inc.: StazOn)
- Silver gel pen (American Crafts: Ultimate Gel Pen)
- Computer and laser printer
- Computer fonts CD (Creating Keepsakes: Creative Lettering Combo)
- Four ¹/₁₆" silver eyelets (Making Memories)
- Double-sided vellum tape (3M: Scotch Vellum Tape)
- Adhesive dots and dispenser (Centis HERMAfix)
- Basic card-making tools (see page 11)
- ¹/₁₆" hole punch
- ³/₄" letter *E* punch (EK Success: Paper Shapers)
- Small dry paint brush
- Eyelet setter
- Hammer
- Heat tool (Marvy Uchida)
- Small scissors

Craft a wedding invitation with style and finesse using your home computer. Crisp laser printing on a vellum overlay makes it easy to create the precise number of invitations that you need. Spend a romantic evening or two with your honey to put it all together.

MI AMOR

10.18.03

Together with their families

REBECCA LILLIAN DAHLKE
&
FRANCISCO DAVID NUNEZ

invite you to join
in their celebration of marriage

OCTOBER EIGHTEENTH
TWO THOUSAND AND THREE
at
HALF-PAST SIX

Ashbury Methodist Church
Janesville, Wisconsin

Reception to foll
1469 Poi

M _____

M _____

_____ Will be attending

_____ Will not be attending

Please respond by September first.

Instructions (for wings invitation)

1. Score and fold the light blue cardstock in half to make a 4" x 5 1/8" card, folded edge at left. (See "Folding Paper" on page 5.)

2. Punch through the blue floral paper using the letter *E* punch. Discard the positive *E* shape. Trim the remaining paper 3/16" beyond the negative *E* cutout to create a border.

3. Photocopy a pair of clip art wings onto white cardstock. Go over the wing lines with a silver gel pen. Cut out each wing with small scissors, leaving a slim margin of white around each one.

 DESIGNER'S TIP

Copyright-free clip art makes an excellent design source for your card making projects. You can find art for every imaginable subject in books and online, ready to scan, resize, and print using your personal computer or a commercial photocopier.

4. Mount the portrait photocopy on the mat board, using the adhesive dots dispenser. Press all four edges of the mounted photo into a gold pigment inkpad. Sprinkle gold embossing powder on the wet ink. Shake off and conserve the excess powder. Use a small, dry paintbrush to remove any lingering particles from the photo. Heat with a heat tool to melt the powder and create an embossed frame around the photo. (See "Embossing" on page 7.)

5. Lay out the 1 3/4" x 1 1/2" music paper and the pieces made in steps 2–4 on the card front, referring to the project photograph for placement. When you are satisfied with your collage placement, mount the pieces with double-sided vellum tape, starting with the piece at the back and working forward.

6. Using a computer, compose your wedding invitation text to fit within a 3 1/8" x 3 3/4" space. Print your text onto vellum using a laser printer. (See "Working with Text" on page 8 and the project photo below, and "Pick a Font" below.)

 PICK A FONT

CK Bella
23-point size

7. Trim the vellum to 3 1/2" x 4 5/8", centering the text. Stamp a dove in black nonporous ink in the lower left corner, overlapping the text if necessary. Allow to dry. Trace over the dove image with a silver gel pen.

8. Center the vellum on the inside of the card. Slip the 3 1/2" x 1 1/2" music paper underneath the vellum and align the top right corners. Remove the vellum. Mount the music print on the card in this position using the adhesive dots dispenser.

9. Reposition the vellum on the card. Punch a hole at each corner, using a 1/16" hole punch. Set a silver eyelet in each hole, using an eyelet setter and a hammer. (See "Installing Eyelets" on page 9.)

Materials (for RSVP card)

- 8$\frac{1}{2}$" x 11" piece of white cardstock
- 8$\frac{1}{2}$" x 11" piece of vellum
- 3$\frac{1}{2}$" x 4$\frac{3}{4}$" piece of light blue cardstock
- 1" x 1" piece of blue floral print paper (Anna Griffin: #AG020)
- Clip art wings (Dover Publications *Early Advertising Alphabets, Initials & Typographic Ornaments*)
- Photocopier service, such as Kinko's
- Computer and laser printer
- Computer fonts CD (Creating Keepsakes: Creative Lettering Combo)
- $\frac{1}{16}$" silver eyelet (Making Memories)
- Double-sided dry tacky tape (Suze Weinberg: Wonder Tape)
- pH neutral PVA bookbinding glue (Books By Hand)
- Silver gel pen (American Crafts: Ultimate Gel Pen)
- Basic card-making tools (see page 11)
- $\frac{1}{16}$" hole punch
- $\frac{3}{8}$" heart punch (EK Success: Folk Heart Paper Shapers)
- Chip brush or flat artist's brush
- Small scissors

Instructions (for RSVP card)

1. Cut a heart-shaped opening in the light blue cardstock, centered $\frac{1}{4}$" above the lower edge, using the heart punch. Attach the blue floral paper to the back of the card, to show through the opening, using double-sided tape.

2. Photocopy a pair of clip art wings onto white cardstock. Go over the lines with a silver gel pen. Cut out each wing with small scissors, leaving a slim margin of white around each one. Brush bookbinding glue on the back of each wing, using a chip brush or flat artist's brush. Mount the wings on each side of the heart.

 PICK A FONT
CK Bella
23-point size

3. Using a computer, compose your RSVP text to fit within a 2$\frac{3}{4}$" x 3" space. Print your text onto vellum using a laser printer. (See "Working with Text" on page 8 and the project photo and "Pick a Font" above.)

4. Trim the vellum to 3" x 3$\frac{3}{4}$", allowing a $\frac{1}{2}$" margin at the top and equal margins at the sides.

5. Place the vellum on the cardstock, allowing a $\frac{3}{16}$" margin at the top and sides. Punch a hole at the top center, $\frac{3}{8}$" from the top edge of the cardstock, using a $\frac{1}{16}$" hole punch. Install a silver eyelet to join the layers.

PICK A FONT

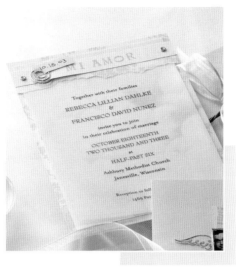

MRS. EAVES SMALL CAPS
20-point: couple's names
18-point: wedding date

Mrs. Eaves Roman
14-point: invitation text
10-point: reception text

Materials (for Mi Amor invitation)

- 8½" x 11" piece of vellum
- 5" x 7" piece of pale pink cardstock
- 6" x 1" strip of pale pink cardstock
- 1¼" x 3/16" piece of pale blue cardstock
- 5" x 7" piece of pink floral paper (Anna Griffin: #AG217)
- 5" x 1" strip of pink floral paper with torn edge on one 5" side (Anna Griffin: #AG217)
- 4⅝" x 6⅝" piece of cloud-patterned paper (Printworks)
- Antique uppercase alphabet rubber stamps (PSX)
- Pink pigment inkpad (Color Box: Mist Petal Point Ink)
- Black fine-tip marker (American Crafts: Slick Writer)
- Computer and laser printer
- Silver circle-shaped clip (Making Memories)
- Two 1/16" copper snaps (Making Memories)
- Adhesive dots and dispenser (Centis HERMAfix)
- Double-sided dry tacky tape (Suze Weinberg: Wonder Tape)
- Basic card-making tools (see page 11)
- 1/16" hole punch
- Eyelet setter
- Hammer

Instructions
(for Mi Amor invitation)

1. Mount the 5" x 7" pink floral paper on the 5" x 7" pale pink cardstock, using the adhesive dots dispenser.

2. Compose your wedding invitation on the computer, sizing the text to fit within a 2¾" x 4½" space and to start 1¾" from the top of the page. Print your text onto vellum using a laser printer. (See "Working with Text" on page 8 and the project photo on page 40, and "Pick a Font" at left.)

3. Trim the vellum to 4⅝" x 6⅝", allowing a 1¾" margin above the text and equal margins at the sides.

4. Turn the cloud paper facedown. Apply a 4½" strip of double-sided tape ½" below the top edge. Center and mount the cloud paper on the pink floral card from step 1. Mount the vellum overlay on the cloud paper in the same way.

5. Stamp *MI AMOR* in pink ink on the pink cardstock strip, using the alphabet rubber stamps. Allow to dry. Trim the cardstock to 5" x 5/8", centering the stamped text. Mount the stamped strip on the pink floral strip, top and side edges aligned, using double-sided tape.

6. Place the layered *MI AMOR* strip across the top of the card, 3/8" below the top edge. Punch a hole at each end of the strip, using a 1/16" hole punch. Install a copper snap at each end, using an eyelet setter and a hammer, to attach the strip to the card. (See "Installing Eyelets" on page 9.)

7. Slip a silver clip onto the lower left edge of the *MI AMOR* strip. Print the wedding date on the 1¼" x 3/16" pale blue cardstock, using a black fine-tip marker, and insert it in the clip.

ANNIVERSARY CARDS 🌿

By Christine Adolph

Materials (for small butterfly card)

- 9¹/₂" x 4³/₄" piece of light blue cardstock
- 3" x 3" piece of gold metallic cardstock
- 1 sheet inkjet-printable canvas (burlingtonpaper.com)
- Clear slide page (Avery: PP22-10, 13404)
- Computer, scanner, and color inkjet printer
- Sewing thread: turquoise, gold
- Gel glue (Golden: Gel Medium)
- Basic card-making tools (see page 11)
- Chip brush
- Sewing machine

Instructions (for small butterfly card)

1. Fold and score the light blue cardstock in half to make a 4³/₄" x 4³/₄" card, folded edge at left. (See "Folding Paper" on page 5.)

2. Brush gel glue on the back of the gold metallic cardstock, using a chip brush. Center and mount the gold cardstock on the card front, pressing to adhere. Allow to dry.

3. Use your computer setup to scan the small butterfly and background text (at right). Print the scanned image in color on inkjet-printable canvas. If you don't have a computer and inkjet printer, you can still print on fabric. Visit a photocopier service and make a color photocopy of your artwork onto heat transfer paper. Then use a warm, dry iron to transfer the image to fabric. Read the heat transfer paper instructions for more details.

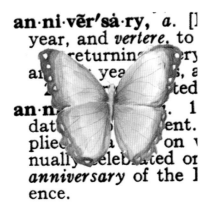

4. Trim the canvas image to 2" x 2". Cut 1 slide sleeve from the clear slide page. Insert the 2" x 2" canvas image into the transparent sleeve.

5. Open the card flat. Center the transparent sleeve on the card front. Drop the feed dogs on the sewing machine. Using turquoise thread, stitch around the edges of the transparent sleeve through all layers to close the sleeve and attach it to the card.

6. Set the sewing machine for a satin stitch (a closely spaced zigzag stitch). Using gold thread, stitch around the outer edge of the gold metallic cardstock. Reset the machine to a straight stitch. Stitch a freestyle looped design in the light blue border.

Two butterfly anniversary cards take their inspiration from the textile arts. Print the colorful butterfly images on a specially prepared canvas, using your computer's inkjet printer. Then mount each image on a card and surround it with playful machine stitching using ordinary sewing threads.

Materials (for large butterfly card)

- 9½" x 4¾" piece of gold metallic cardstock
- 8½" x 11" piece of inkjet-printable canvas (burlingtonpaper.com)
- 8½" x 11" piece of transparency film
- Thin script background text rubber stamp (A Stamp in the Hand: Q1771)
- Gold foil (Anita's Foil Leafing)
- Liquid foil adhesive (Anita's Foil Leafing)
- Blue acrylic paint (Delta Ceramcoat "Ocean Reef Blue")
- White acrylic paint (Delta Ceramcoat "White")
- Computer, scanner, and color inkjet printer
- Photocopier service, such as Kinko's
- Sewing thread: turquoise, gold metallic
- Gel glue (Golden: Gel Medium)
- Basic card-making tools (see page 11)
- Artist's brush
- Chip brush
- Scrap of cardstock
- Sewing machine
- Small disposable container
- Wooden craft stick

Instructions (for large butterfly card)

1. Fold and score the gold metallic cardstock in half to make a 4¾" x 4¾" card, folded edge at left. (See "Folding Paper" on page 5.)

2. Photocopy the dictionary *anniversary* text (at right) onto transparency film. Cut the film about ¼" beyond the text all around, making a 3" x ⅞" piece.

3. Use your computer setup to scan the large butterfly image (at right). Print the butterfly in color on inkjet-printable canvas. Tear the canvas into a 4" x 4" square, centering the butterfly.

4. Mix small amounts of blue and white acrylic paint together to make light blue, using a wooden craft stick and a disposable container. Brush the paint on the canvas around the butterfly, using an artist's brush. Make random, overlapping strokes for a textured,

mottled appearance. Allow some of the canvas to show through. Allow to dry.

 DESIGNER'S TIP

Practice the foil stamping technique on scrap paper first, before stamping on fabric. Apply the foil adhesive sparingly to avoid losing detail in the stamp.

5. Cut a butterfly shape from scrap cardstock for a mask. Lay the mask over the printed butterfly. Apply liquid foil adhesive to the rubber stamp, using a chip brush. Stamp the canvas. The mask will prevent the adhesive from touching the butterfly. Brush adhesive around the outer edges of the canvas, taking one or two strokes on each edge.

6. As soon as the adhesive is dry, place a sheet of foil, metallic side up, on top of the canvas. Rub lightly with your finger to adhere. See the manufacturer instructions for additional information. Some foils require heat to adhere.

7. Drop the feed dogs on the sewing machine. Using turquoise thread, machine stitch two or three times around the outer edge of the canvas. Center the transparency film from step 2 under the butterfly. Using gold metallic thread, stitch once around the text through both layers, about ⅛" in from the edge.

8. Brush gel glue on the back of the canvas. Center the butterfly canvas on the card front and press to adhere. Allow to dry.

THANK-YOU CARDS

By Cindi Nelson

Materials (for pink striped card)

- 3½" x 5" pink striped note card (Savvy Stamps)
- 3" x 3" piece of white water-color paper (Savoir Faire)
- 2¼" x 2¼" piece of olive green cardstock with torn edges
- Square block rubber stamp (Savvy Stamps: 320F)
- Pressed daisy rubber stamp (Savvy Stamps: 184F)
- Pink pigment inkpad (VersaColor: Petal Pink)
- Sepia, plum, and dusty pink water-based brush pens (Marvy LePlume II Markers #45, #64, and #66)
- Water brush pen (EK Success: Zig Brush H2O)
- 5" length of pink fiber ribbon (Making Memories: Funky Fibers)
- Tacky glue (api Crafter's Pick: The Ultimate!)
- Basic card-making tools (see page 11)

Create these three "watercolor" cards without paints. Ink your stamps with water-based brush pens. Then use a water brush pen on the stamped paper to spread and dissipate the colors. For another soft watercolor look, stamp three flowers without re-inking.

Instructions (for pink striped card)

1. Stamp a square block in pink ink onto watercolor paper.

2. Color the pressed daisy stamp with the brush pens. Use a sepia pen for the daisy center and the words *thank you*. Use a plum pen for the petal outlines and dusty pink for the interiors. Stamp onto the pink color block made in step 1.

3. Fill the water brush pen with water. Rub the water brush pen over the individual daisy colors. The paper will allow the ink to flow, creating a watercolor effect. Allow to dry.

4. Cut out the image a scant ⅛" beyond the pink block outline. Glue the image to the green cardstock.

5. Attach the ribbon to the front of the note card, parallel to and 1¼" from the folded edge, using a dot of glue at each end.

6. Glue the layered panel to the card front, ⅝" from the folded edge and 1" from the top edge, overlapping the ribbon.

1. Fold and score the 8" x 10" watercolor paper in half, to make a 4³/8" x 6³/4" card, folded edge at left. (See "Folding Paper" on page 5.)

2. Stamp the striped background in pink ink onto the 3¹/4" x 5" watercolor paper about ¹/2" from the top and side edges.

3. Color the butterfly stamp with the water-based brush pens. Use a sepia pen for the butterfly body. Use a plum pen for the wings outline and dusty pink for the interior. Stamp a butterfly at a slight angle onto the striped background prepared in step 2.

4. Fill the water brush pen with water. Rub the water brush pen over the individual butterfly colors to blend the colors on the paper. Allow to dry.

5. Stamp *THANK YOU* in brown ink below the butterfly, letting the words and dash line trail off the striped background.

6. Glue the stamped paper to the light olive green cardstock a scant ¹/8" from the top edge, ¹/4" from each side edge, and ³/8" from the bottom edge. Allow to dry.

7. Punch a ¹/8" hole, centering it ³/8" from the top edge. Thread the gingham ribbon through the hole. Tie the ribbon ends together in a double knot. Trim the tails at an angle.

8. Glue the layered panel to the card front, about ³/8" from the top and side edges and 1" from the bottom edge.

Materials (for butterfly card)

- 8⁷/8" x 6³/4" piece of natural watercolor paper (Savoir Faire)
- 3¹/4" x 5" piece of ivory watercolor paper with torn edges (Savoir Faire)
- 3⁵/8" x 5¹/2" piece of light olive green cardstock
- Stripe background rubber stamp (Savvy Stamps: 159J)
- Butterfly rubber stamp (Savvy Stamps: 301F)
- Trailing *THANK YOU* rubber stamp (Savvy Stamps: 305F)
- Pink pigment inkpad (VersaColor: Petal Pink)
- Brown pigment inkpad (VersaColor: Pinecone)
- Sepia, plum, and dusty pink water-based brush pens (Marvy LePlume II Markers #45, #64, and #66)
- Water brush pen (EK Success: Zig Brush H20)
- 4" length of chartreuse gingham ribbon, ³/16" wide (May Arts)
- Glue stick or rubber cement
- Basic card-making tools (see page 11)
- ¹/8" hole punch

Materials (for floral trio card)

- 5¹/₂" x 4¹/₄" (size A-2) light mauve note card
- 3⁵/₈" x 2¹/₈" pink vellum envelope (Impress)
- 3⁹/₁₆" x 2¹/₁₆" piece of white cardstock
- 2¹/₄" x 2¹/₂" piece of white cardstock
- 1⁹/₁₆" x 1⁵/₁₆" piece of dark olive green cardstock
- *thank you* background rubber stamp (Savvy Stamps: 228G)
- *thanks for everything* rubber stamp (Savvy Stamps: 221E)
- Daisy rubber stamp (Savvy Stamps: 174D)
- Brown pigment inkpad (Versacolor: Pinecone)
- Green and plum water-based brush pens (Marvy LePlume II Markers #64 and #96)
- Rubber cement or glue stick
- Basic card-making tools (see page 11)

 DESIGNER'S TIP

To tone down a crisply stamped image, lay a piece of vellum over it or slip it inside a vellum envelope.

Instructions (for floral trio card)

1. Stamp the *thank you* background in brown ink onto the 3⁹/₁₆" x 2¹/₁₆" white cardstock. Let the words go right up to and beyond the edges. Allow to dry. Insert the card into the vellum envelope. Set aside.

2. Color the daisy stamp with the water-based brush pens. Use a green pen for the stem and leaves. Use a plum pen for the flower. Stamp a daisy onto the middle of the 2¹/₄" x 2¹/₂" white cardstock. Without re-inking, stamp one daisy to the left and one daisy to the right, letting the petals overlap the center daisy. The two side daisies will appear muted. Allow to dry.

3. Cut the stamped cardstock to measure 1⁷/₁₆" x 1³/₁₆", centering the daisies. Sketch a rectangular border freehand around the daisies, using the green brush pen.

4. Glue the daisy piece, centered, to the green cardstock. Glue the layered panel to the envelope, sealing the envelope flap. Glue the envelope to the front of the note card, allowing a ¹⁵/₁₆" margin at the top and side edges and a 1³/₁₆" margin at the lower edge.

5. Stamp *thanks for everything* in brown ink on the card front, centered ³/₈" below the envelope.

MOTHER'S DAY CARDS 🪶

By Christine Adolph

Materials (for daisy card)

- 9¹/₂" x 4³/₄" piece of bright pink cardstock
- 4" x 4"* piece of white cardstock
- 3¹/₄" x 3³/₄"* piece of bright yellow cardstock
- 4" x 5"* piece of sheet music
- 8¹/₂" x 11" piece of transparency film
- Photocopier service, such as Kinko's
- Acrylic paints: green, yellow, white (Delta Ceramcoat)
- Crackle medium
- Sewing thread: magenta, green
- Gel glue (Golden: Gel Medium)
- Basic card-making tools (see page 11)
- Assorted artist's brushes
- Chip brush
- Scalloped edge scissors
- Sewing machine

*Approximate size; cut freehand

Instructions (for daisy card)

1. Fold and score the bright pink cardstock in half to make a 4³/₄" x 4³/₄" card, folded edge at left. (See "Folding Paper" on page 5.)

2. Brush gel glue on the back of the sheet music, using a chip brush or flat artist's brush. Mount the sheet music on the card front off-center, to create an irregular bright pink border. Glue the yellow cardstock to the sheet music in the same way, creating an irregular music print border. Allow to dry.

3. Paint the white cardstock green and yellow, using an artist's brush. Allow to dry. Following the manufacturer's instructions, brush crackle medium over the surface in crisscrossed strokes, using a flat artist's brush. Allow to dry 20 to 40 minutes, or until surface becomes tacky. Paint the entire surface white. Almost immediately, the white paint will seize up and form cracks, revealing the yellow and green base coat underneath. Allow to dry.

4. Trim the crackled cardstock to approximately 3" x 3¹/₄", using scalloped edge scissors. Test-fit the piece on your collage, retrimming if necessary to create an irregular bright yellow border all around. Glue in place. Allow to dry.

5. Photocopy the daisy/dictionary text (at right) onto transparency film. Cut out the image freehand, making a rectangle that measures approximately 2¹/₂" x 2³/₄".

Flower images copied onto transparent film let you peer clear through to the crackle-patterned paper underneath. Music papers add a lovely grace note to these Mother's Day collages. Use music papers printed for scrapbooking or hunt down vintage sheet music at tag sales and antique shops. Cut the collage papers freehand for a playful look.

mŏth′ẽr

6. Open the card flat. Place the transparent piece from step 5 on the card front, slightly off-center. Drop the feed dogs on the sewing machine. Using green thread, stitch around the edges of the transparent film through all layers. You will be able to see through the flower to the crackle pattern underneath.

7. Reset the sewing machine for a zigzag stitch. Using green thread, zigzag around the edges of the sheet music. Using magenta thread, zigzag around the edges of the yellow cardstock.

Materials (for rose card)

- 9¹/₂" x 4³/₄" piece of bright yellow cardstock
- 3¹/₄" x 3¹/₄"* piece of white cardstock
- 3" x 3¹/₄"* piece of bright pink cardstock
- 4" x 4" piece of sheet music
- Photocopier service, such as Kinko's
- 8¹/₂" x 11" piece of transparency film
- Acrylic paints: green, white (Delta Ceramcoat)
- Crackle medium
- Sewing thread: magenta, green
- Gel glue (Golden: Gel Medium)
- Basic card-making tools (see page 11)
- Assorted artist's brushes
- Chip brush or flat artist's brush
- Scalloped edge scissors
- Sewing machine

*Approximate size; cut freehand

 DESIGNER'S TIP

As an alternative to sewing, install an eyelet at each corner of a transparency to secure it to the card.

Instructions (for rose card)

1. Fold and score the bright yellow cardstock in half to make a 4³/₄" x 4³/₄" card, folded edge at left. (See "Folding Paper" on page 5.)

2. Brush gel glue on the back of the sheet music, using a chip brush or a flat artist's brush. Adhere the paper to the card front off-center, to create an irregular bright yellow border. Glue the bright pink cardstock to the sheet music in the same way, creating an irregular music print border. Allow to dry.

3. Paint the white cardstock green, using an artist's brush. Allow to dry. Following the manufacturer's instructions, brush crackle medium over the surface in crisscrossed strokes. Allow to dry 20 to 40 minutes, or until surface becomes tacky. Paint the entire surface white. The white paint will seize up and form cracks, revealing the green base coat underneath. Allow to dry.

4. Trim the crackled cardstock to approximately 2³/₄" x 2³/₄", using scalloped edge scissors. Test-fit the piece on your collage, retrimming if necessary to create an irregular bright pink border all around. Glue in place. Allow to dry.

5. Photocopy the rose/dictionary text (below) onto transparency film. Cut out the image freehand, making a rectangle that measures approximately 2³/₈" x 2¹/₂".

6. Open the card flat. Place the transparent piece from step 5 on the card front, slightly off-center. Drop the feed dogs on the sewing machine. Using green thread, stitch around the edges of the transparent film through all layers.

7. Reset the sewing machine for a zigzag stitch. Using magenta thread, zigzag around the edges of the sheet music.

nŭr'tŭre

FATHER'S DAY CARDS 🍃

By Saralyn Ewald
Creative Coordinator for
Archiver's—The Photo
Memory Store

Materials (for photo card)

- 11" x 5½" piece of buff textured cardstock
- 3" x 5½" piece of brown velvet paper
- 3⅛" x 2⅝" piece of mat board
- 4" x 5" piece of clear acetate
- 3⅛" x 2⅝" black-and-white photo (dimensions include white border)
- Ruler sticker (Nostalgiques by Rebecca Sower: Rule of Thumb)
- Burgundy pigment inkpad (VersaColor)
- Silver paint pen
- Four ⅛" pewter eyelets (Making Memories)
- Gold metallic embroidery thread

- Double-sided dry tacky tape (Suze Weinberg: Wonder Tape)
- Transparent tape (3M: Scotch Magic Tape 811)
- pH neutral PVA bookbinding glue (Books By Hand)
- Spray adhesive (3M: Super 77)
- Basic card-making tools (see page 11)
- Chip brush or flat artist's brush
- Crewel needle
- Eyelet setter (Making Memories)
- Hammer
- Paper piercer
- ⅛" hole punch (Making Memories)

A multimedia approach is sure to win smiles from Dad. These Father's Day cards make the most of masculine collage elements. An old-fashioned ruler, metal eyelets, wire mesh, a boyhood photo, and tiles from his favorite word game capture his personality to a T. He can use the tags later on to help spot his luggage at the airport.

Instructions (for photo card)

1. Score and fold the buff cardstock in half to make a 5½" x 5½" card, folded edge at left. (See "Folding Paper" on page 5.)

2. Score and fold the brown velvet paper in half lengthwise. Brush bookbinding glue on the back, using a chip brush or flat artist's brush. Mount the brown velvet piece on the card, aligning the folds and top and bottom edges, to form a spine.

3. Open the card flat. Pierce a series of holes in the card front, about ⅛" apart, as shown in the diagram. Using a crewel needle and gold metallic thread, hand-sew a running stitch through the holes. Tape down the thread ends on the inside front cover, using transparent tape.

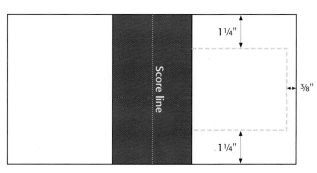

4. Write a few words on the clear acetate with a silver paint pen. Allow to dry. Make a few straight cuts across the corners of the acetate to create a random shape. Press a burgundy pigment inkpad onto the acetate, using it like a sponge to print overlapping blocks of color. Allow some of the stampings to go over the edge.

5. Spray the inked side of the acetate (ink can still be wet) with spray adhesive. Place the acetate on the card front, inked side down, butting one edge against the spine and overlapping the gold stitching in some places. Press to adhere.

6. Center a ruler sticker over the spine/acetate join, parallel to the spine fold. Press to adhere. Trim the ends of the sticker even with the top and bottom edges of the card.

7. Mount the photo on the mat board using spray adhesive. Punch a hole in each corner of the mounted photo, using a 1/8" hole punch. Set an eyelet in each hole, using an eyelet setter and hammer. (See "Installing Eyelets" on page 9.)

8. Mount the photo on the card front within the gold metallic stitching lines, using double-sided tape.

 DESIGNER'S TIP

Book binding glue provides a smooth finish and flexibility. It prevents the adhered paper from wrinkling as the card opens and closes.

Materials (for linked tags)

Two 2¹/₂" x 4³/₄" manila tags

1⁷/₈" x 1¹/₂" piece of red cardstock with torn edge on one 1⁷/₈" side

Page from an antique book

Scrap of brown velvet paper

Scrap of mat board

1¹/₂"-diameter metal-rimmed white tag (Making Memories)

Wooden tile alphabet stickers (Making Memories)

2" alphabet stencils (U.S. Stamp & Sign: 2" Gothic Caps Stencil Kit)

Antique uppercase alphabet stamps (PSX)

Watermark inkpad (VersaMark)

Jet black inkpad (Tsukineko Co. Staz On)

Acrylic paints: red, orange, yellow, brown

2¹/₄" x 2³/₄" piece of wire mesh

Bead chain (Making Memories)

24-gauge silver wire

Two ¹/₈" gold eyelets (Making Memories)

Double-sided dry tacky tape (Suze Weinberg: Wonder Tape)

Transparent tape (3M: Scotch Magic Tape 811)

Vellum adhesive tape

pH neutral PVA bookbinding glue (Books By Hand)

Tacky glue (api Crafter's Pick: The Ultimate!)

Basic card-making tools (see page 11)

¹/₈" hole punch (Making Memories)

⁹/₁₆" circle punch

Assorted artist's brushes

Eyelet setter (Making Memories)

Hammer

Jewelry pliers

Paper piercer (Making Memories)

Wire cutters

Instructions (for linked tags)

1. Dab a watermark inkpad directly onto both sides of the manila tags, to create a weathered appearance. Allow to dry.

2. Punch two ⁹/₁₆" circles from a scrap of brown velvet paper. Glue a circle to each tag over the existing hole, using bookbinding glue.

3. Punch a hole through each velvet circle, to correspond to the tag's hole, using a ¹/₈" hole punch. Set a gold eyelet in the hole, using an eyelet setter and a hammer. (See "Installing Eyelets" on page 9.)

DAD TAG

1. Using wire cutters, cut off three corners of the wire mesh to make a free-form shape. Place the wire mesh on the middle of one tag, the uncut corner at the top right, as shown in the project photo (at right).

2. Cut a 2" piece of silver wire, using wire cutters. Bend the wire into a hairpin shape. Pierce two closely spaced holes in the tag on either side of a mesh wire, using a paper piercer. Insert the hairpin ends through the holes. Use pliers to pull through and twist both ends together on the underside. Clip the wire ends, leaving a 1/2" tail. Bend the tail flat against the tag and tape down with vellum adhesive tape. Repeat this process to secure the wire mesh in several locations.

3. Align the red cardstock along the left edge of the tag, torn edge at the bottom and partially covering the wire mesh. Adhere the cardstock to the tag in this position, using double-sided tape against the paper and tacky glue against the wire mesh.

4. Select wooden tile stickers to spell *DAD*. Cut and affix a slightly smaller piece of cardstock to the back of each sticker. Apply the stickers to the red cardstock using bookbinding glue. The extra backing will raise the stickers off the surface, for a dimensional look.

5. Pierce a line of closely spaced holes parallel to and 5/16" from the lower edge of the tag, using a paper piercer.

POP TAG

1. Tear the page of text, making a curved edge. Select the paper with the convex curve for your tag. Test-fit the paper on the tag, referring to the project photo (above).

2. Brush bookbinding glue on the wrong side of the paper. Mount the paper on the tag so that the curved edge runs across the tag and the paper hangs off the left edge and part of the bottom edge. Allow to dry. Trim off the excess paper even with the edges of the tag, using an X-Acto knife.

3. Place the 2" *P* stencil on a scrap of white paper. Trace lightly with a pencil. Remove the stencil. Paint the *P* red and orange, using an artist's brush. Allow to dry.

4. Use an X-Acto knife to trim the painted *P* to 1" x 1 5/8", cropping off the right side of the letter. Brush bookbinding glue on the wrong side of the letter. Mount the letter sideways on the lower left corner of the tag, as shown in the project photo (above).

5. Place the 2" *O* stencil on the tag, to the left of the *P*, top edges aligned. Trace lightly with a pencil. Remove the stencil. Paint the *O* red and orange, using an artist's brush. Allow to dry.

6. Trim the actual *P* stencil to 1 3/4" x 2". Shade the interior edges with a pencil for more definition. Cut and affix short strips of mat board to the back, using double-sided tape. Glue the *P* stencil to the tag using bookbinding glue. Overlap the *O* slightly and let the stencil's lower edge hang slightly off the edge of the tag. The mat board strips on the back will raise the stencil up off the surface, for a dimensional look.

Final Assembly

1. Paint the paper portion of a metal-rimmed tag with yellow and brown paint, using an artist's brush. Allow to dry.

2. Stamp *MY HERO* in black ink on one side of the tag, using the antique alphabet rubber stamps. Allow to dry.

3. Run a bead chain through all three tags and lock closed.

MOVING ANNOUNCEMENTS

*By Saralyn Ewald
Creative Coordinator for
Archiver's—The Photo
Memory Store*

Materials (for square card)

- 5" x 10" piece of pale green speckled cardstock
- 2½" x 2½" piece of green accounting paper with one torn edge (Ampad: Columnar Pad)
- 6" length of 2"-wide brown packing tape, torn from roll
- Paint chip strip for olive greens
- Antique wooden uppercase and lowercase alphabet type
- Black dye-based inkpad (Clearsnap Inc.: Ancient Page Dye Ink in Coal Black)
- White acrylic paint
- 2" antique skeleton key
- 3" length of burgundy chenille flat yarn (On the Surface Embellishments: Victorian Dreams VDT124)

- Double-sided dry tacky tape (Suze Weinberg: Wonder Tape)
- Removable adhesive tape (3M: Scotch Magic Tape 811)
- Adhesive dots and dispenser (Centis HERMAfix)
- pH neutral PVA bookbinding glue (Books By Hand)
- Basic card-making tools (see page 11)
- ⅛" "anywhere" hole punch
- Chip brush
- Eraser
- Flat artist's brush
- Soft lead pencil
- Tracing paper

New address? No problem. Friends and family will know you've unpacked your craft supplies when you send these clever announcements. Collage elements on the square card include a paint chip strip, packing tape, and a skeleton key. Striped and crackled scrapbook papers look like wallpaper on a house-shaped cutout.

Instructions (for square card)

1. Score and fold the cardstock in half to make 5" x 5" card, folded edge at left. (See "Folding Paper" on page 5.)

2. Brush bookbinding glue on the back of the packing tape, using a chip brush. Mount the packing tape along the left edge of the card, slightly askew, so one torn edge shows at bottom and the tape runs off the card at the left and top edges. Fold the excess tape at the left onto the back of card. Allow to dry. Trim the excess tape at the top even with the edge of the card.

3. Fold the paint chip strip lengthwise, right side out and slightly askew. Unfold and lay flat. Brush bookbinding glue on the back, using a chip brush. Slip the strip around the card, aligning the folds, to create a spine. Press to adhere. Allow to dry. Trim the excess at the top and bottom even with the edges of the card.

4. Mount the green accounting paper on the card front, 1" from the top edge and 3/4" from the right edge, with the torn edge at the bottom, using the adhesive dots dispenser.

5. Enlarge the house (below) and use a soft lead pencil to trace it onto tracing paper. Place the tracing facedown on the card front, overlapping the accounting paper and brown tape as desired. Tape down with removable tape. Go over the sketch with the pencil, pressing firmly to transfer the lines. Remove the tracing.

6. Go over the transferred drawing with the pencil. Add lines, to suggest a rough sketch rather than a finely detailed drawing. Soften the pencil lines by rubbing them with an eraser. Brush white acrylic paint over the drawing using a flat artist's brush. Make long brushstrokes that follow the lines of the architecture.

7. Stamp *We MOVed* in black ink across the top of the card, letting the letters extend beyond edge.

8. Open the card flat. Place the skeleton key on the card front, at the lower right, as shown in the project photo (page 58). Mark and punch two holes on either side of the key shaft, using a 1/8" hole punch. Thread the chenille yarn through the holes. Mount the key on the card using a thin strip of double-sided tape. Then tie the yarn ends around the key.

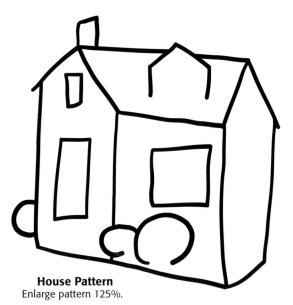

House Pattern
Enlarge pattern 125%.

Materials (for cutout card)

- 8" x 8" piece of olive cardstock
- 5" x 5" piece of olive striped paper (Anna Griffin: #AG204)
- 2¾" x 4" piece of beige crackle-pattern paper with torn edge on one 2¾" side (Creative Imaginations, Debbie Mumm)
- ¾" x 4½" piece of bronze metallic cardstock
- Scrap of kraft-colored cardstock
- 1⅛" x 1⅛" gold filigree corner sticker (Class A'Peels: Victorian Borders)
- 3¾" gold skeleton leaf
- ¼" antique bronze rivet (Chatterbox Rivets: #91014)
- 1¼" green medallion faux wax seal (Creative Imaginations, Sharon Soneff)
- Double-sided dry tacky tape (Suze Weinberg: Wonder Tape)
- pH neutral PVA bookbinding glue (Books By Hand)
- Basic card-making tools (see page 11)
- ¼" hole punch
- Chip brush
- Template plastic

Instructions (for cutout card)

1. Enlarge and trace the house card pattern (page 61) onto template plastic. Cut out the template. Trace around the template with a pencil to mark 1 house card on olive cardstock. Cut out the shape. Also cut the interior solid lines, as indicated on the pattern. Score and fold the cutout shape on the dotted line, to make an asymmetrical card, folded edge at left. (See "Templates" on page 6 and "Folding Paper" on page 5.)

2. Open the card flat. Slip a piece of scrap template plastic on the card back, under the roofline of the card front, as a mask. Brush bookbinding glue on the back of the striped paper, using a chip brush. Mount the striped paper at an angle on the upper half of the card front, as shown in the project photo (page 58). The mask will protect the back of the card. Allow to dry. Trim off the excess paper even with the edge of the card.

3. Open the card flat and mask the card back with plastic, as in step 2. Brush bookbinding glue on the back of the crackle-pattern paper, using a chip brush. Mount the paper on the card front, a straight edge even with the fold and the torn edge overlapping the striped paper at an angle. Allow to dry. Trim off the excess.

4. Carefully brush bookbinding glue on the back of the skeleton leaf, using a chip brush. Mount the leaf on the card front, with the leaf spine parallel to and $7/8$" from the fold. Apply the gold filigree sticker to the lower left corner, partially overlapping the leaf.

5. Cut the bronze cardstock strip in half. Hold both strips together, edges even. Slip the folded card in between, allowing the excess strip to extend evenly at each end. Grip

firmly and turn the entire sandwich over. Without releasing your grip, trim the back strip even with the folded edge. Fold the front strip onto the back. Glue down both strips to the back of the card, using bookbinding glue. Allow to dry.

6. Turn the card right side up. Punch a hole through the two remaining strip ends, as close to the card edge as possible, using a $1/4$" hole punch. Open the card and write your message inside. Close the card and set a bronze rivet through the hole to secure the ends. Trim off the excess strip at a slight angle.

7. Mount the faux wax seal on the kraft-colored cardstock, using double-sided tape. Make a single straight tear in the cardstock about $1/8$" from the seal. Cut the remaining three edges close to the seal to make an asymmetrical four-sided shape. Mount the seal and its cardstock backing to the card front to left of the rivet, using double-sided tape. If you like, enclose a skeleton key with your card to "open" the lock.

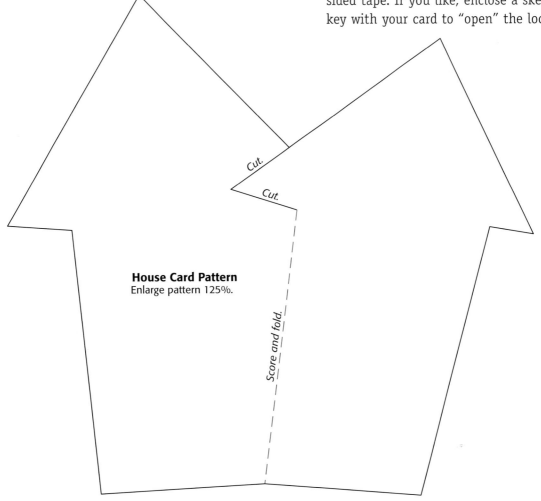

House Card Pattern
Enlarge pattern 125%.

you take the cake

happy birthday

make a wish

BIRTHDAY CAKE CARDS 🌿

By Cindi Nelson

Materials (for polka-dot cake card)

- 4¼" x 5½" (size A-2) light chartreuse note card (Savvy Stamps)
- 3¼" x 3¾" piece of white cardstock
- 2¾" x 3¼" piece of olive green textured paper with torn edges
- Pinstripe background rubber stamp (Savvy Stamps: 252G)
- *happy birthday* background rubber stamp (Savvy Stamps: 328G)
- 1⅞" x 2⅜" scalloped frame rubber stamp (Savvy Stamps: 258H)
- Polka-dot cake rubber stamp (Savvy Stamps: 325E)
- *you take the cake* rubber stamp (Savvy Stamps: 329C)
- Soft gray-green pigment inkpad (VersaColor: Laurel)
- Yellow-green pigment inkpad (VersaColor: Bamboo)
- Brown pigment inkpad (VersaColor: Pinecone)
- Four ⅛" silver mini-brads (Making Memories)
- Basic card-making tools (see page 11)
- Paper piercer

Multiple stampings create these birthday cake collages. stamp the backgrounds first in soft ink colors. Then use brown ink to add your favorite chocolate cake.

Instructions (for polka-dot cake card)

1. Stamp a pinstripe background in gray-green ink on the middle of the white cardstock.

2. Stamp a *happy birthday* background in yellow-green ink on top of the pinstripe background.

3. Stamp a scalloped frame in brown ink around the backgrounds.

4. Stamp a polka-dot cake in brown ink, centering it within the frame.

5. Trim the white cardstock to 2¼" x 2¾", or about ³/₁₆" beyond the stamped frame all around.

6. Open the note card flat. Place the olive green paper on the front of the card, about ⅝" from the top edge, ¾" from the fold and the right edge, and 1½" from the bottom. Center the white cardstock on the olive green paper. Pierce a small hole at each corner of the white cardstock through all three layers. Insert a silver mini-brad through each hole. Press back and flatten the prongs on the other side.

7. Stamp *you take the cake* in brown ink on the card front, centered below the attached panel.

Materials (for triple-tiered cake card)

- 4¼" x 5½" (size A-2) medium chartreuse note card
- 2¼" x 2½" piece of white cardstock
- 2⁵/₁₆" x 3" piece of olive green textured paper, with torn edge on one 2⁵/₁₆" side
- 2⁵/₁₆" x 3¼" piece of taupe textured paper, with torn edge on one 2⁵/₁₆" side
- Square block rubber stamp (Savvy Stamps: 320F)
- Stripe block rubber stamp (Savvy Stamps: 308F)
- Cake tower rubber stamp (Savvy Stamps: 332E)
- *make a wish* rubber stamp (Savvy Stamps: 218C)
- Soft gray-green pigment inkpad (VersaColor: Laurel)
- Yellow-green pigment inkpad (VersaColor: Bamboo)
- Brown pigment inkpad (VersaColor: Pinecone)
- Rubber cement
- Basic card-making tools (see page 11)

Instructions (for triple-tiered cake card)

1. Stamp a square block in gray-green ink on the white cardstock, ¼" in from the top and side edges.

2. Stamp a stripe block in yellow-green ink directly over the square block, to create a subtle striped background.

3. Stamp a cake tower in brown ink on the background, letting the cake stand extend off the background about ³/₈".

4. Brush rubber cement on the back side of the taupe paper and onto the middle of the card front. When both applications reach tack, mount the taupe paper on the note card, torn edge at the bottom and about 1" in from the top and side edges. Glue the olive paper to the taupe paper in the same way, top and side edges aligned. Glue the stamped white cardstock to the olive paper,

allowing a ¹/₁₆" margin around the top and side edges.

5. Stamp *make a wish* in brown ink on the card front, centered below the attached panel.

Materials (for circle tag card)

- 3½" x 5" yellow-striped note card (Savvy Stamps)
- 1⁷/₈"-diameter metal-rimmed white tag (Making Memories)
- Circle polka-dot block rubber stamp (Savvy Stamps: 322E)
- Cake plate rubber stamp (Savvy Stamps: 297E)
- *happy birthday* rubber stamp (Savvy Stamps: 330C)
- Yellow-green pigment inkpad (VersaColor: Bamboo)
- Brown pigment inkpad (VersaColor: Pinecone)
- 5" length of chartreuse braid, ¼"-wide (May Arts)
- Rubber cement
- Basic card-making tools (see page 11)
- Chip brush

Instructions (for circle tag card)

1. Stamp a polka-dot circle in yellow-green ink in the center of the rimmed tag.

2. Stamp a cake plate in brown ink over the stamped circle, letting the long cake stand legs touch the tag's silver rim.

3. Thread the braid through the tag hole and tie the ends in a knot.

4. Brush rubber cement on the back of the tag and onto the card front, about 1" in from the top and side edges. When both applications reach tack, mount the tag on the card front, ³/₄" from the top edge and ⁵/₈" from each side.

5. Stamp *happy birthday* in brown ink, centered below the tag and 1½" above the card's lower edge.

BABY SHOWER INVITATION AND THANK-YOU CARD 🦋

By Dawn Anderson

Materials (for invitation)

- 8¹/₂" x 11" piece of baby blue vellum
- 5" x 11" piece of baby blue cardstock with torn edge on one 5" side
- 4" x 5" piece of yellow fiber paper
- 3" x 5" piece of baby blue mulberry paper with fibers
- 2" x 2" piece of cream paper cut with a deckle paper edger
- 1¹/₂" x 1¹/₂" piece of cream paper
- 1"-diameter metal-rimmed baby blue vellum tag (Making Memories)
- 1³/₄" x 1³/₄" blue vellum sticker with musical notes (Mrs. Grossman's Paper Company: Audrey Giorgi and Maria Ayala: Vellum Medallions)
- Baby carriage rubber stamp (Savvy Stamps: 339D)
- Blue dye-based inkpad (Uchida Marvy Matchables "Salvia Blue")
- Computer and laser printer
- *baby* eyelet word (Making Memories)
- Square pewter alphabet charms
- 1¹/₈ yards of yellow fuzzy thread (Rainbow Gallery: Wisper)
- Acid-free double-sided tape (Therm O Web: Mounting Tape)
- Double-sided vellum tape (3M: Scotch Vellum Tape)
- Adhesive dots sheets (Therm O Web: Sticky Dots)
- Tacky glue (api Crafter's Pick: The Ultimate!)
- Basic card-making tools (see page 11)
- ¹/₈" "anywhere" hole punch
- Eyelet setter
- Hammer

Metal accents turn ordinary invitations and thank-you notes into keepers for the scrapbook. Use alphabet charms to spell out key words. A shiny baby rattle charm glued to the front of a card leaves no doubt about the subject of your thank-you note.

DESIGNER'S TIP

If you use an inkjet printer, you won't be able to print directly onto vellum—the ink will bleed or rub off. To get around the problem, print your message onto regular copy paper and then photocopy it onto vellum at a photocopy shop.

Instructions (for invitation)

1. Lay the baby blue cardstock flat, torn edge at the left. Mount the yellow fiber paper on the baby blue cardstock, aligning the top, right, and bottom edges, using double-sided mounting tape. Mount the baby blue mulberry paper to the left of the yellow fiber paper, using an adhesive dots sheet.

2. Score and fold the cardstock in half to make a 5¹/₂" x 5" card, folded edge at left. (See "Folding Paper" on page 5.) The torn blue edge should peek out from behind the yellow edge at the right. The blue mulberry paper will form a spine.

Thank You

baby

You're invited to a Shower

B O Y

3. Wrap fuzzy thread around card front about seven times to embellish the area where the yellow and blue papers join. Tie the thread ends together on the inside front cover and trim the tails.

4. Using a computer, type the message *You're invited to a Shower*, leaving 1³/₁₆" space between the words *a* and *Shower*. To match the project card, use the Lucida Calligraphy font in 16-point size. Print onto vellum. Trim the message to ¹/₂" x 5".

5. Mount the message strip on the card front, centered down the blue mulberry spine, using double-sided vellum tape. Punch a hole in the center of the metal-rimmed vellum tag, using a ¹/₈" hole punch. Install the *baby* eyelet word on the tag, using an eyelet setter and a hammer. (See "Installing Eyelets" on page 9.) Glue the tag to the vellum strip with tacky glue to complete the message.

6. Stamp a baby carriage in blue ink on the 1¹/₂" x 1¹/₂" cream paper, centering the design. Center and mount the blue vellum sticker on the cream paper with deckle-cut edges. Center and mount the carriage image on the vellum sticker, using double-sided tape. Mount the carriage label on the card front, 1" from the top and side edges of the yellow paper, using double-sided mounting tape.

7. Arrange three pewter alphabet charms under the carriage label to spell *BOY*. Angle the *B* and the *Y* outward at the top. Secure with tacky glue.

Materials (for thank-you card)

- 4¹/₄" x 6" pink checked note card (Marcel Schurman Creations)
- 8¹/₂" x 11" piece of pink mottled cardstock
- 2" x 2" piece of cream cardstock cut with a deckle paper edger
- 2¹/₄" x 2¹/₄" square of baby blue pearlescent cardstock
- Computer and printer

- 1³/₄" x 1³/₄" pink vellum sticker (Mrs. Grossman's Paper Company: Audrey Giorgi and Maria Ayala: Vellum Medallions)
- Silver rattle charm (Westrim Crafts Paper Bliss: Baby Accents)
- ¹/₄ yard of baby blue silk ribbon, ¹/₄"-wide
- 5" length of pink silk ribbon, ⁵/₁₆"-wide
- Acid-free double-sided tape (Therm O Web: Mounting Tape)
- Tacky glue (api Crafter's Pick: The Ultimate!)
- Basic card-making tools (see page 11)

Instructions (for thank-you card)

1. Using a computer, type *Thank You*, leaving a 1¹/₂" border on the left and a 3³/₄" border on the top. To match the project card, use the Lucida Calligraphy font in 18-point size. Print onto pink mottled cardstock. (See "Working with Text" on page 8.)

2. Trim the printed cardstock to 4¹/₄" x 4⁷/₈", centering the words *Thank You* 1" above the bottom edge. Mount the cardstock on the card front, top and side edges aligned, using double-sided tape.

3. Mount the pink ribbon along the lower edge of the cardstock, bordering the pink checked band, using double-sided tape. Wrap and adhere the ends of the ribbon to the back and inside of the card.

4. Center and mount the vellum sticker on the cream cardstock with deckle-cut edges. Center and mount this deckle-cut piece on the baby blue square, using double-sided tape. Mount the entire layered piece on the card front, ⁵/₈" from the upper edge and 1" from the side edges, using double-sided tape.

5. Slip the rattle charm onto the blue ribbon. Tie the ribbon in a bow and trim the tails at an angle. Glue the rattle charm to center of pink sticker label, using tacky glue. Allow to dry.

Baby *boy*

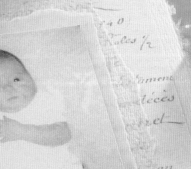

BABY

JEFFRE

Announcing:

Isabelle Marie
Date: June 15, 2003
Time: 12:56 pm
Weight: 8 lb. 6 oz.
Length: 20"

BIRTH ANNOUNCEMENTS 🌿

By Dawn Anderson

Materials (for blue card)

- 4¼" x 11" piece of baby blue pearlescent cardstock
- 3¾" x 4¼" piece of baby blue mulberry paper with fibers
- 1¼" x 1⅛" black-and-white or sepia-tone photocopy of baby
- *Baby* script rubber stamp (K DeNami Design)
- Silver pigment inkpad (Color Box)
- Silver embossing powder (PSX)
- Pewter *boy* eyelet word (Making Memories)
- 1⅜" x 1¼" silver frame with rope edging (Nunn Design)
- 1⅛ yards of baby blue textured thread
- 9" length of baby blue silk ribbon, ¼"-wide
- Adhesive dots sheet (Therm O Web: Sticky Dots)
- Tacky glue (api Crafter's Pick: The Ultimate!)
- Basic card-making tools (see page 11)
- ⅛" "anywhere" hole punch
- Eyelet setter
- Hammer
- Heat tool

Pink or blue, either of these cards introduces a new family member to the world. Make the cards ahead of time if you like—perhaps as a baby shower craft activity—and then add your photos as soon as the stork makes a delivery!

Instructions (for blue card)

1. Score and fold the cardstock in half to make a 4¼" x 5½" card, folded edge at top. (See "Folding Paper" on page 5.)

2. Mount the mulberry paper on the card front, side and bottom edges aligned, using an adhesive dots sheet. Wrap textured thread five times around card front over the paper seam. Tie the thread ends together on the inside front cover and trim the tails.

3. Stamp *Baby* with silver pigment ink on the card front, centered within the pearlescent rectangle at the top of the card. Sprinkle silver embossing powder onto the wet ink. Shake off and conserve the excess powder. Heat with a heat tool to melt the powder and emboss the surface. (See "Embossing" on page 7.)

4. Open the card flat. Punch a hole in the card front, ½" in from the right and lower edges of the pearlescent rectangle, or just below and to the right of the stamped letter *y*, using a ⅛" hole punch. Install the *boy* eyelet word, using an eyelet setter and a hammer. (See "Installing Eyelets" on page 9.)

5. Mount the photo in the frame. Thread ribbon through the frame's metal loop and tie in a bow. Trim the ribbon tails at an angle. Center and mount the frame on the mulberry paper section of the card front using tacky glue.

Materials (for pink card)

- 5" x 6¼" ivory note card with deckled edge
- 8½" x 11" piece of ivory cardstock
- 2¼" x 6¼" piece of pink mottled cardstock
- 2½" x 3¼" piece of pink cardstock with torn edge on one 2½" side
- 3⅝" x 6¼" piece of French ledger paper (7 Gypsies: Franc)
- 3" x 6¼" piece of pink sheer paper with torn edge on one 6¼" side (Magenta Maruyama Paper: Soft Pink 6001)
- 2¼" x 3¼" piece of pink vellum with torn edges
- 2" x 2⅞" black-and-white or sepia-tone photo
- ¼" x 6¼" piece from a pink scallop-edge sticker (Mrs. Grossman's Paper Company: Julie Cohen & Melissa K. Carlson: Linen Pink Ribbon Paper Whispers)
- Pink acid-free chalk (EK Success: Nursery Rhymes Chalklets)
- Computer and printer
- Square pewter alphabet charms
- Mesh heart eyelet (Making Memories)
- Silver ⅛" eyelet (Making Memories)
- ¾ yard of pink silk ribbon, ⁵⁄₁₆"-wide
- 7" length of pink textured thread (Rainbow Gallery: Fuzzy Stuff)
- Acid-free double-sided tape (Therm O Web: Mounting Tape)
- Adhesive dots sheet (Therm O Web: Sticky Dots)
- Tacky glue (api Crafter's Pick: The Ultimate!)
- Basic card-making tools (see page 11)
- ⅛" "anywhere" hole punch (Making Memories)
- Chalk applicator tool (Pazzles)
- Eyelet setter (Making Memories)
- Hammer
- Template plastic

Instructions (for pink card)

1. Color the deckled edge of the premade card with pink chalk, using the applicator tool.

2. Fold the mottled pink cardstock in half lengthwise. Mount it on the card spine with double-sided tape, aligning the folds and edges. Mount the French ledger paper on the card front to the right of the spine, allowing the deckled edge to peek through at the right.

3. Mount the pink sheer paper on the ledger paper with an adhesive dots sheet, aligning the long straight edge with the spine. Apply a pink scallop-edge sticker along the right edge of the spine, so that the scalloped edge overlaps the sheer paper.

4. Mount the vellum on the card front, 1¾" to the right of the folded edge, 2" from the upper edge, and 1¼" from the lower edge, using double-sided tape. Center and mount the photo on the vellum, using double-sided tape.

5. Open the card flat. Punch a hole at the lower right corner of the photo, using a ⅛" hole punch. Install a mesh heart eyelet, using an eyelet setter and a hammer. (See "Installing Eyelets" on page 9.)

6. Compose your birth announcement on the computer, sizing the text to fit within a 1³/₈" x 1³/₈" print area. Print onto ivory cardstock. (See "Working with Text" on page 8, the project photo on page 68, and "Pick a Font" at right.)

7. Trace the small and large tag patterns (below) onto template plastic. Cut out both templates. Place the smaller template on the computer printout and trace the tag outline. Use the larger template to mark an outer tag with a torn lower edge on the 2¹/₂" x 3¹/₄" pink cardstock. Cut out both tags. (See "Templates" on page 6.)

8. Mount the printed tag on the pink tag with double-sided tape, creating an even pink border around the upper and side edges. Punch a hole at the top of the tag, using a ¹/₈" hole punch. Set a silver eyelet in the hole, using an eyelet setter and a hammer. (See "Installing Eyelets" on page 9.) Run pink textured thread through the eyelet and knot the ends together.

9. Open the card flat. Wrap pink ribbon around the card front, alongside the folded edge. Tie a single knot, slip on the looped tag thread, and complete by tying a bow.

10. Arrange four pewter alphabet charms on the card front, about ⁷/₈" from the upper edge, to spell *BABY*. Angle the *B's* to the left and the *A* and the *Y* to the right. Secure with tacky glue.

PICK A FONT
Lucida Calligraphy

12-point: the word Announcing

10-point: baby's name and birth facts

8-point: the words Date, Time, Weight, *and* Length.

DESIGNER'S TIP

For an alternative to pewter alphabet charms and eyelet words, try alphabet stickers or alphabet rubber stamps. You can also create your own adhesive letters using your computer. Print the desired letters on plain or colored paper, cut out the letters in the desired shape, and apply double-sided tape to the back.

Tag Patterns

ALL-OCCASION
HEART CARDS

By Christine Adolph

Materials (for small heart card)

- 9½" x 4¾" piece of gold metallic cardstock
- 4¾" x 4" piece of blue print paper (Dick Blick)
- 4⅜" x 3½"* piece of papyrus (Dick Blick)
- 3¼" x 2¼"* piece of blue striped batik paper (see "Making Wax Resist Batik Paper" on page 75)
- 2½" x 3"* piece of tan corrugated paper (Dick Blick)

- Old book
- Turquoise sewing thread
- Gel glue (Golden: Gel Medium)
- Basic card-making tools (see page 11)
- Chip brush
- Sewing machine
- Template plastic

Approximate size; cut freehand

Create your own striped batik papers for these cards, using the designer's easy method (page 75). To streamline your card making, substitute one of the many beautiful hand silk-screened or batik papers available on-line or at your local art store. Either way, the quirky, irregular shapes that you cut freehand keep the collage process relaxed and fun.

Instructions (for small heart card)

1. Fold and score the gold metallic cardstock in half to make a 4¾" x 4¾" card, folded edge at left. (See "Folding Paper" on page 5.)

2. Brush gel glue on the back of the blue print paper, using a chip brush. Center and mount the paper on the card front, allowing an equal margin of gold metallic paper to show at the top and bottom edges. Press to adhere.

3. Brush glue on the back of the papyrus. Mount the papyrus on the card front, a bit off-center, to create an irregular blue border. Press to adhere. Mount the blue striped batik paper on the papyrus in the same way.

4. Trace the small heart pattern (page 75) onto template plastic. Cut out the template. Trace around the template with a pencil to mark 1 heart on corrugated paper. Cut out the heart. (See "Templates" on page 6.)

5. Center and mount the heart on the card front, 1½" from each edge, using gel glue. Allow to dry.

6. Select and cut out 7 individual capital letters from the old book to spell *CHERISH*. Lay out the letters on the papyrus, below the heart, spacing them about ¼" apart. Glue in place, using gel glue. Allow to dry.

7. Open the card flat. Drop the feed dogs on the sewing machine. Using turquoise thread, machine stitch through all layers, just inside the outer edges of each piece. Alternate between zigzag and straight stitch.

Materials (for large heart card)

- 9¹/₂" x 4³/₄" piece of light blue cardstock
- 4³/₄" x 4³/₄" piece of blue print paper (Dick Blick)
- 3¹/₂" x 4"* piece of tan corrugated paper (Dick Blick)
- 1" x 4"* piece of gold metallic paper
- Two ⁷/₈" x 4"* pieces of blue striped batik paper (see "Making Wax Resist Batik Paper" on page 75)
- Old book
- Turquoise sewing thread
- Gel glue (Golden: Gel Medium)
- Basic card-making tools (see page 11)
- Chip brush
- Sewing machine
- Template plastic

Approximate size; cut freehand

Instructions (for large heart card)

1. Fold and score the light blue cardstock in half to make a 4³/₄" x 4³/₄" card, folded edge at left. (See "Folding Paper" on page 5.)

2. Brush gel glue on the back of the blue print paper, using a chip brush. Center and mount the paper on the card front.

3. Brush glue on the back of the gold metallic paper. Mount the gold metallic paper on the blue print paper, parallel to and ³/₈" from the right edge of the card.

4. Brush glue on the back of one batik paper. Mount the batik paper on the gold paper, allowing a slim margin of gold to show at the right.

5. Brush glue on the back of the corrugated paper. Mount the corrugated paper on the card front, overlapping the left edge of the blue batik paper. Allow a ³/₈" margin at the top, bottom, and left edges of the card.

6. Test-fit the remaining blue batik strip on the corrugated paper, lining up the top, bottom, and left edges. Trim the right edge to contour the shape, as shown in the project photo (above). Glue in place.

7. Trace the large heart pattern (page 75) onto template plastic. Cut out the template. Trace around the template with a pencil to mark 1 heart on blue batik paper. Cut out the heart. (See "Templates" on page 6.)

8. Brush gel glue on the back of the heart. Mount the heart on the card front, close to the right and bottom edges of the corrugated paper. Allow to dry.

9. Select and cut out 4 individual capital letters from the old book to spell *LOVE*. Lay out the letters on the large heart, midway between the top and bottom edges of the card, spacing them about ¹/₄" apart. Glue in place, using gel glue. Allow the entire card to dry.

10. Open the card flat. Drop the feed dogs on the sewing machine. Using turquoise thread, machine stitch through all layers, just inside the outer edges of each piece. Use straight stitch on the heart and zigzag stitch everywhere else.

MAKING WAX RESIST BATIK PAPER

Materials

- Tableau rice paper (Dick Blick)
- Turquoise concentrated watercolor (Dr. Ph. Martin's Radiant Concentrated Watercolor)
- Wax (Nasco Arts and Crafts)
- Chip brush
- Watercolor brush
- Double boiler or wax melting pot (Nasco Arts and Crafts)
- Newsprint
- An old iron
- Small disposable cup

Instructions

1. Cover your work surface with newsprint.

2. Melt the wax in a double boiler on the stovetop or in an electric wax melting pot. Wax is combustible; do not leave the wax unattended or overheat it. Once the wax is melted, turn down the temperature. Keep the wax warm and in a liquid state.

3. Dip a chip brush into the liquid wax and immediately brush it onto a sheet of rice paper. Try out different patterns with your brush: stripes, dots, curves. Dip a cork into the wax and stamp with it. Allow the wax on the paper to cool and harden. Make sure the paper doesn't stick to the work surface.

4. Dispense a few drops of concentrated watercolor into a small cup. Dilute with water to the desired color. Brush the color onto the paper, using a watercolor brush. Allow to dry.

5. Sandwich the batik paper between several layers of newsprint. Press with a warm, dry iron to melt and remove the wax. Repeat as needed.

Heart Patterns

EXPLORE

dream

LIVE

R E T I R E

As you venture toward a new horizon...

RETIREMENT CARDS ❦

By Sonya Anderson
Instructor for Archiver's—
The Photo Memory Store

Materials (for mixed media card)

- 5½" x 11" piece of cypress green cardstock
- 5¼" x 10¾" piece of ivory cardstock
- 2" x 2½" piece of ivory cardstock
- ⅞" x 1¾" piece of ivory cardstock
- 3" x 3" piece of handmade textured paper (Creative Papers Online)
- 1" x 5" piece of kraft-colored cardstock
- 1" x 4" piece of kraft-colored cardstock
- Wooden tile alphabet stickers (Making Memories)
- 3" x 7½" brown self-adhesive mesh (Advant Card: Magic Mesh)
- Printer's type uppercase alphabet rubber stamps (Hero Arts)
- Woodblock alphabet rubber stamps (Hero Arts)
- *CONGRATULATIONS* rubber stamp (Hero Arts)
- Wheat dye-based inkpad (Hero Arts Shadow Ink: Soft Wheat)
- Black inkpad (Tsukineko: Brilliance Ink)
- Seven ¼" silver brads (Making Memories)
- Sticker letters for brads (Creative Imaginations: Impress-ons Bradwear)
- Pewter *dream* eyelet word (Making Memories)
- Silver 1⅛" x 1¾" eyelet frame (Making Memories)
- Six ½" pewter eyelets (Making Memories)
- 3" length of thin jute
- Double-sided adhesive tabs and dispenser (Centis HERMAfix)
- Basic card-making tools (see page 11)
- 1" x 1⅝" plastic tag template (Deluxe Designs)
- ⅛" "anywhere" hole punch (Making Memories)
- ¹⁄₁₆" "anywhere" hole punch (Making Memories)
- Paper piercer
- Eyelet setter
- Hammer

Retirement isn't the end; it's the beginning. Get your friends and family members of a certain age off to a good start with cards that spell out the possibilities. Who knows? You might jump-start a second career in card making!

Instructions (for mixed media card)

1. Score and fold the cypress cardstock in half to make a 5½" x 5½" card, folded edge at left. Score and fold the 5¼" x 10¾" ivory cardstock in half to make a slightly smaller card liner. (See "Folding Paper" on page 5.)

2. Place the square of handmade paper on the card front at an angle, ⅝" from the top edge, ⅛" from the right edge, 1" from the bottom edge, and 1½" from the folded edge, as shown in the project photo (page 76). Mount in place using adhesive tabs.

3. Open the card flat. Place the self-adhesive mesh on the card front, parallel to and ¼" to the right of the fold. Fold the excess mesh at the top and bottom edges onto the reverse side.

4. Press individual letters onto 7 silver brads to spell *explore*. Pierce a hole at the top left corner of the card front, ¾" from the top edge and ¾" from the fold, using a paper piercer. Insert an *e* brad into the hole. Flatten the prongs on the reverse side. Pierce 6 more holes, about ⅜" apart, and install the remaining brads. Vary the spacing from the top edge of the card for a playful look.

5. Trace around the plastic template with a pencil to mark a tag on the 2" x 2½" ivory cardstock. Cut out the tag. Pierce a hole at the top, using the ¹⁄₁₆" hole punch. Stamp a *D* in wheat ink on the tag, slightly off-center, using a woodblock rubber stamp. Hitch a 3" length of jute through the hole.

6. Mount the tag on the handmade paper, ⅜" in from the right and top edges, using adhesive tabs. Punch a hole through the tag and cardstock, using a ⅛" hole punch. Install the *dream* eyelet word, using an eyelet setter and a hammer. (See "Installing Eyelets" on page 9.)

7. Stamp *LIVE* in black ink in the middle of the ⅞" x 1¾" ivory cardstock. Trim the cardstock as needed to fit behind the silver eyelet frame. Place the frame and cardstock on the card front at an angle, ⅜" from the fold and 1⅛" from the bottom edge. Punch a hole at each corner of the frame, using a ⅛" hole punch. Install 4 pewter eyelets, using an eyelet setter and a hammer. (See "Installing Eyelets" on page 9.)

8. Apply wooden tile stickers side by side to the 1" x 4" kraft-colored cardstock to spell *RETIRE*. Trim the cardstock a scant ¹⁄₁₆" beyond the stickers. Mount the strip on the lower right corner of the card front using adhesive tabs.

9. Mount the liner from step 1 inside of card, centered and with folds aligned, using adhesive tabs.

10. Stamp *CONGRATULATIONS* in black ink on the 1" x 5" kraft-colored cardstock. Trim the cardstock to 3½" x 1", centering the word. Open the card to the inside. Center the strip on the inside panel, 2⅛" below the top edge. Punch a hole at each end of the strip, using a ⅛" hole punch. Install pewter eyelets, using an eyelet setter and a hammer. (See "Installing Eyelets" on page 9.)

Materials (for photo card)

- 8½" x 11" piece of sage cardstock
- 5½" x 11" piece of blue-gray cardstock
- 2" x 5½" piece of beige handmade textured paper with torn edge on one 5½" side (Creative Papers Online)
- 4" x 4" sepia-tone beach photo
- 1¼" x 1¼" sepia-tone beach photo, plus photo scraps after cutting
- 1½" x 1½" metal-rimmed white tag (Making Memories)
- Computer and inkjet printer
- Extra computer fonts (CK Fresh Fonts CD)
- Two ³/₁₆" pewter eyelets (Making Memories)
- Two ⅛" pewter eyelets (Making Memories)
- 2 oval page pebbles (Making Memories)
- 3 small starfish (Magic Scraps)
- Double-sided adhesive tabs and dispenser (Centis HERMAfix)
- Glue dots (Memory Book)
- pH neutral scrapbook glue (Magic Scraps: Scrappy Glue)
- Basic card-making tools (see page 11)
- Chip brush
- ³/₁₆" "anywhere" hole punch (Making Memories)
- ⅛" "anywhere" hole punch (Making Memories)
- Eyelet setter
- Hammer

Instructions (for photo card)

1. Score and fold the blue-gray cardstock in half to make a 5½" x 5½" card, folded edge at top. (See "Folding Paper" on page 5.)

2. Mount the handmade paper on the card front at the top, using adhesive tabs and aligning the long straight edge with the card fold.

3. Using a computer, type *As you venture toward a new horizon....* To match the project card, use the CK Constitution font (available on the CK Fresh Fonts CD) in 20-point. Print the file onto sage cardstock. Trim the cardstock to 5½" x ½", centering the message. (See "Working with Text" on page 8.)

4. Open the card flat. Place the 4" x 4" beach photo on the card front at an angle, so that the top left corner is ¼" from the left edge and the top right corner is ¼"" from the fold. Punch a hole at each top corner of the photo, ¼" in from the edges, using a ³/₁₆" hole punch. Install a ³/₁₆" eyelet in each hole, using an eyelet setter and a hammer. (See "Installing Eyelets" on page 9.)

5. Run the message strip from step 3 across the bottom of the card, parallel to and ⁵/₁₆" above the bottom edge, and slightly overlapping the photo. Punch a hole at each end of the strip, ¼" from the card edge, using a ⅛" hole punch. Install a ⅛" eyelet in each hole, using an eyelet setter and a hammer. (See "Installing Eyelets" on page 9.)

6. Mount the 1³/₈" x 1³/₈" photo on the square tag, using adhesive tabs. Mount the tag at an angle on the lower right of the card front with glue dots. Let the tag overlap the larger photo and a bit of the message strip.

7. Adhere the oval page pebbles to some photo scraps. Trim off the excess, even with the edge of the pebble. Mount the pebbles on the card front as shown in the project photo (above) or as desired, using adhesive tabs.

8. Add starfish to the card front using scrapbook glue.

BOO

HAPPY HALLOWEEN

HALLOWEEN PARTY INVITATIONS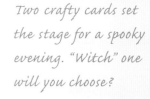

By Dawn Anderson

Materials (for card with tag)

- 4³/4" x 6³/4" piece of ivory paper with French black script (7 Gypsies: Large Script)
- 4³/4" x 7¹/2" piece of orange ribbed cardstock
- 4³/4" x 2" piece of orange cardstock
- 3" x 4" piece of orange cardstock
- 3" x 4" piece of black cardstock
- 1¹/2" x 8¹/4" piece of black mulberry paper with fibers, torn on one long edge
- 4³/4" x 8¹/4" piece of orange mesh (Magenta Maruyama Paper "Pumpkin Nest")
- Black typewriter alphabet stickers (Nostalgiques by Rebecca Sower: Black Typewriter ABC)
- Haunted house rubber stamp (Hero Arts)
- Black dye-based inkpad (Memories)
- 3 small silver conchos from typewriter key words (7 Gypsies: Journal Jewelry)
- ³/4"-diameter circle-shaped clip (Making Memories)

- ¹/8" black eyelet (Making Memories)
- 24-gauge silver spool wire
- 6 mm jump ring
- 3 medium blank page pebbles (Making Memories)
- 1 vial size 11 silver-lined crystal seed beads
- 1 vial size 8 black seed beads
- Five 6 mm orange bicone beads
- Acid-free double-sided tape (Therm O Web: Mounting Tape)
- Adhesive dots sheet (Therm O Web: Sticky Dots)
- Foam adhesive dots (All Night Media Mini: Pop Dots)
- Basic card-making tools (see page 11)
- Round-nose pliers
- Template plastic
- Wire cutter
- ¹/8" "anywhere" hole punch
- Eyelet setter
- Hammer

Two crafty cards set the stage for a spooky evening. "Witch" one will you choose?

1. Score the 4³/₄" x 2" orange cardstock length-wise, dividing it into a ³/₄"-wide section and a 1¹/₄"-wide section. Do not fold. Apply a strip of double-sided tape to the 4³/₄" edge of the wider section. Adhere the orange cardstock to one end of the ivory printed paper, overlapping the edges by about ¹/₂", or so the entire piece measures 8¹/₄" long.

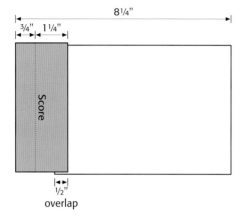

2. Lay the orange/ivory rectangle flat with the orange cardstock at the top. Mount the black mulberry paper on the orange/ivory rectangle, top and left side edges aligned, using an adhesive dots sheet. Mount orange mesh over the entire piece, using an adhesive dots sheet.

3. Turn the rectangle over. Apply double-sided tape to the ³/₄"-wide section of the orange piece. Mount the orange ribbed cardstock to the taped section, for the card back. Fold the card in half along the score line made in step 1 to make a 4³/₄" x 7¹/₂" card.

4. Trace the individual tag patterns (at right) onto template plastic. Cut out both templates. Stamp a haunted house in black ink on the 3" x 4" orange cardstock, about ¹/₂" above the lower edge. Place the smaller tag template on top so that the haunted house falls at the bottom of the tag. Trace around the tag outline. Place the larger tag template on the 3" x 4" black cardstock and trace the outline. Cut out both tags. (See "Templates" on page 6.)

5. Center and mount the orange tag on the black tag using double-sided tape. Punch a hole in the top of the tag through both layers, using a ¹/₈" hole punch. Install a black eyelet, using an eyelet setter and a hammer. (See "Installing Eyelets" on page 9.)

6. Cut a 5" length of silver wire. Make a double coil at one end, using round-nose pliers. Thread on 2 silver-lined seed beads, 1 black bead, 1 orange bead, and 1 black bead. Repeat five times, then finish with 2 more silver-lined beads. Trim the wire ⁵/₈" beyond final bead. Make a double coil to end off.

7. Join one end of the bead chain to a jump ring. Join the jump ring to the tag eyelet. Attach the other end of the bead chain to the circle clip. Slip the clip over folded edge at the top of the card.

8. Select three sticker letters to spell out *BOO*. Adhere one letter, right side up and centered, to the back of each page pebble. Trim off the excess even with the pebble edge. Place each page pebble inside a round silver concho. Insert two foam adhesive dots from the back. Set the *B* concho on the lower right corner of the card front, 2¹/₄" from the right edge and 1¹/₄" from the lower edge. Press the rivets into the card. Press in the points on the back side with the eraser end of a pencil. Repeat for the remaining letters, spacing the conchos a scant ¹/₄" apart.

Tag Patterns

Materials (for pumpkin card)

- 6³/₈" x 9¹/₄" piece of black ribbed paper
- 4" x 5³/₄" piece of orange flecked cardstock
- 2" x 2⁷/₈" piece of French printed paper (7 Gypsies: Grenoble)
- 2³/₈" x 3³/₈" piece of black paper with torn edges
- ¹/₂" x 4" piece of orange vellum
- Scrap of black paper
- 2" x 5³/₄" piece of orange mesh (Magenta Maruyama Paper "Pumpkin Nest")
- *Happy Halloween* rubber stamp (Savvy Stamps: 273C)
- Black dye-based inkpad (Memories)
- Green metal paint
- ⁷/₈" orange pumpkin charm
- Black eyelets
- Green-wrapped floral wire
- Ultra-fine orange pearlescent glitter (Barbara Trombley's Art Glittering System "Tang")
- Clear adhesive for glitter (Barbara Trombley's Art Glittering System: "Dries Clear" Adhesive)
- Acid-free double-sided tape (Therm O Web: Mounting Tape)
- Adhesive dots sheet (Therm O Web: Sticky Dots)
- 3-D clear adhesive dots (Therm O Web: 3-D Zots)
- Fabric glue (Beacon: Fabritac)
- Basic card-making tools (see page 11)
- ¹/₈" "anywhere" hole punch (Making Memories)

- Assorted artist's brushes
- Darning needle
- Eyelet setter (Making Memories)
- Hammer
- Wire cutter

Instructions (for pumpkin card)

1. Paint stem of pumpkin charm green, using metal paint and a small artist's brush. Allow to dry. Brush clear adhesive over body of pumpkin, using a round artist's brush. Sprinkle with ultra-fine orange glitter. Shake off and conserve the excess. Set aside to dry.

2. Score and fold the black ribbed paper in half to make a 4⁵/₈" x 6³/₈" card, folded edge at left. (See "Folding Paper" on page 5.)

3. Center and mount the orange cardstock on the card front, using double-sided tape. Adhere the orange mesh to the left side of the orange cardstock, using adhesive dots and aligning the edges.

4. Center and mount the French printed paper on the black paper with torn edges, using double-sided tape. Mount this layered piece on the card front, about ³/₄" from the top edge and 1¹/₈" from the side edges, using double-sided tape.

5. Stamp *Happy Halloween* in black ink on the center of the orange vellum strip. Position the strip on the card front, about 2³/₄" above the lower edge and even with the orange cardstock at the sides. Open the card flat. Punch a hole at each end of the message strip through all layers, using a ¹/₈" hole punch. Install black eyelets to secure the layers, using an eyelet setter and a hammer. (See "Installing Eyelets" on page 9.)

6. Cut a 3" length of floral wire. Insert the wire into the hole at the top of the charm and twist to secure. Coil the wire ends around a darning needle to make curly tendrils. Seal the ends with dot of fabric glue. Allow to dry.

7. Cut a ¹/₂" circle from a scrap of black paper and affix an adhesive dot to one side. Press the adhesive against the back of the pumpkin charm (the black paper shows through the glue dot, filling in the jack o' lantern face). Use another dot to adhere the charm to the French print paper, about ¹/₂" in from the top and side edges.

RED-AND-GREEN CHRISTMAS CARDS

By Dawn Anderson

Materials (for gift card)

- 3⁷/₈" x 12³/₄" piece of red cardstock with torn edge on one 3⁷/₈" side
- 3¹/₂" x 5⁷/₈" piece of light grass green cardstock
- 1¹/₂" x 5" piece of cream cardstock
- 1¹/₂" x 1⁵/₈" piece of cream cardstock
- 1³/₄" x 1⁷/₈" piece of red cardstock
- 1¹/₈" x 3¹/₂" piece of grass green mulberry paper with fibers
- Present rubber stamp (Savvy Stamps: 188E)
- *joy* rubber stamp (Savvy Stamps: 90B)
- Scroll border rubber stamp (Savvy Stamps: 30175F)
- Cranberry pigment inkpad (Color Box)
- Red metallic embossing powder (Ranger Industries: Red Tinsel)
- ¹/₂" x ¹³/₁₆" silver metal tag charm
- ⁵/₈ yard red *Merry Christmas* ribbon (Midori)

- Red metallic fine braid #8 (Kreinik)
- Acid-free double-sided tape (Therm O Web: Mounting Tape)
- Adhesive dots (Therm O Web: All-Purpose Zots)
- Adhesive dots sheet (Therm O Web: Sticky Dots)
- Basic card-making tools (see page 11)
- ¹/₈" "anywhere" hole punch (Making Memories)
- Darning needle
- Paper piercer
- Heat tool

Add glittery highlights to your holiday cards with metallic embossing powder. An embossed metal tag charm and tiny red rhinestones give you more ways to capture and spread the light.

Instructions (for gift card)

1. Fold the 3⁷/₈" x 12³/₄" red cardstock in half to make a 3⁷/₈" x 6³/₈" card, folded edge at top, torn lower edge on card front.

2. Center and mount the light grass green cardstock on the card front, using double-sided tape. Mount the grass green mulberry paper on the light green cardstock, bottom and side edges aligned, using an adhesive dots sheet.

3. Stamp a present in cranberry ink on 1¹/₂" x 1⁵/₈" cream cardstock, allowing ¹/₄" margin all around. Sprinkle red metallic embossing powder onto the wet ink. Shake off and conserve the excess powder. Heat with a heat tool to melt the powder and emboss the surface. (See "Embossing" on page 7.)

4. Repeat step 3 to stamp and emboss a scroll border on the 1¹/₂" x 5" cream cardstock. Trim to ¹/₂" x 3¹/₂".

5. Repeat step 3 to stamp and emboss *joy* on the metal tag charm, as shown in the project photo (above).

 DESIGNER'S TIP

A metal tag will become quite hot during the embossing process. Use a tool that does not conduct heat to hold it secure as you work.

6. Center and mount the embossed package on the 1³/₄" x 1⁷/₈" red cardstock, using double-sided tape. Pierce a hole through both layers at base of bow.

7. Cut a 5" length of red braid. Knot one end. Insert braid through hole in metal tag charm so knot lodges on back. Thread free end in darning needle. Insert needle through pierced hole and draw through until 1" of braid remains on front. Tape down braid on reverse side, trimming off the excess.

8. Mount the layered piece from step 7 on the card front, 1³/₈" from the upper edge and 1" from each side, using double-sided tape. Attach the metal tag charm to the card, as shown in the project photo (page 84), using an adhesive dot. Mount the embossed scroll border strip from step 4 directly above the mulberry paper, using double-sided tape.

9. Open the card flat. Punch two holes in the card front, centered ¹/₂" apart and ³/₄" from the fold, using a ¹/₈" "anywhere" hole punch. Thread the *Merry Christmas* ribbon through the holes from reverse side. Tie in a bow on the card front, adjusting so *Merry* falls on the bow's left loop and *Christmas* falls on the right loop. Trim the tails at an angle.

Materials (for tree card)

- $6^7/8$" x 10" piece of light grass green cardstock
- $4^1/4$" x $6^1/8$" piece of red cardstock
- $2^1/4$" x $3^3/8$" piece of red cardstock with four torn edges
- 4" x $5^7/8$" piece of grass green mulberry paper
- 4" x $5^7/8$" piece of grass green cardstock
- 2" x 3" piece of cream cardstock
- Christmas tree rubber stamp (Savvy Stamps: 91123F)
- Wavy *MERRY CHRISTMAS* rubber stamp (Savvy Stamps: 265C)
- Cranberry pigment inkpad (Color Box)
- Red metallic embossing powder (Ranger Industries: Red Tinsel)
- Light green ink pen (Tombow: AT 195)
- Red ink pen (Tombow: AT 856)
- 1 package size $1^3/4$ mm red Austrian rhinestones (Westrim Crafts)
- Acid-free double-sided tape (Therm O Web: Mounting Tape)
- Adhesive dots sheet (Therm O Web: Sticky Dots)
- Tacky glue (api Crafter's Pick: The Ultimate!)
- Basic card-making tools (see page 11)
- Heat tool

Instructions (for tree card)

1. Score and fold the light grass green cardstock in half to make a 5" x $6^7/8$" card, folded edge at left. (See "Folding Paper" on page 5.)

2. Center and mount $4^1/4$" x $6^1/8$" red cardstock on the card front, using double-sided tape.

3. Mount the grass green mulberry paper on the grass green cardstock, using adhesive dots. With the mulberry paper side up, center and mount this piece on the card front, using double-sided tape.

4. Color the Christmas tree stamp with the ink pens. Use a light green ink pen for the wide stripes and trunk. Use a red ink pen for the narrow stripes. Do not ink the star. Stamp a

tree onto cream cardstock, $1/2$" from the upper edge, $5/8$" from the lower edge, and $1/4$" from each side.

5. Clean the tree stamp thoroughly. Apply cranberry pigment ink to star of tree stamp. (Mask the tree portion of the stamp with tape if necessary.) Align the stamp over the previously stamped tree and stamp a star. Sprinkle red metallic embossing powder onto wet ink. Shake off and conserve the excess powder. Heat with a heat tool to melt the powder and emboss the surface. (See "Embossing" on page 7.)

6. Stamp *MERRY CHRISTMAS* in cranberry ink onto cream cardstock below the tree.

7. Press or rub the cranberry pigment inkpad onto the edges of the $2^1/4$" x $3^3/8$" red cardstock, making a $1/2$" border all around. Sprinkle with red metallic embossing powder onto wet ink. Shake off and conserve the excess. Heat with a heat tool to melt the powder and emboss the surface.

8. Center and mount the stamped tree onto red cardstock, using double-sided tape. Glue red rhinestones to the tree, as shown in the project photo (above), using tacky glue. Allow to dry.

9. Mount the tree piece on the card front, $1^1/4$" from the top and side edges, using double-sided tape.

merry christmas

wishing you

christmas

joy

BLUE-AND-SILVER CHRISTMAS CARDS

*By Sonya Anderson
Instructor for Archiver's—
The Photo Memory Store*

Materials (for photos card)

- 8½" x 11" piece of white cardstock
- 5½" x 8½" piece of blueberry cardstock
- 5¼" x 8¼" piece of white speckled cardstock
- 2⅜" x 1⅛" piece of blue denim cardstock
- 2" x 2" piece of blue denim cardstock
- 3⅞" x 4⅞" piece of white speckled handmade paper (Creative Papers Online)
- Two 1¼" x 1¼" black and white photos
- Two 1½" x 1½" metal-rimmed white tags (Making Memories)
- Snowflake rubber stamp (Inkadinkado: 1689.P)
- Tinted embossing inkpad (Top Boss)
- Silver embossing powder (Ranger Industries)
- Computer and inkjet printer

- Extra computer fonts (CK Fresh Fonts CD)
- Fine-point black permanent pen (Zig: Millenium)
- *Christmas* eyelet word (Making Memories)
- ⅝" pewter snowflake charm (Making Memories)
- Two ⅛" pewter eyelets (Making Memories)
- Tape runner (Hama tape roller)
- Double-sided adhesive tabs and dispenser (Centis HERMAfix)
- Glue dots (Memory Book)
- pH neutral scrapbook glue (Magic Scraps: Scrappy Glue)
- Basic card-making tools (see page 11)
- ⅛" "anywhere" hole punch
- Eyelet setter
- Hammer
- Heat tool

Try this blue and silver palette for a snowy-fresh look. A handcrafted version of the annual family photo card lets you share two candid snapshots. Or design an imaginative land-scape, where a tower of presents and a shimmering tree reach sky-high.

Instructions (for photos card)

1. Score and fold the blueberry cardstock to make a 5½" x 4¼" card, folded edge at top. Score and fold the white speckled cardstock to make the slightly smaller card liner. (See "Folding Paper" on page 5.)

2. Cut the handmade paper diagonally in half to make two triangles. Mount one triangle on the lower left corner of the card front, corners aligned, using adhesive tabs.

3. Use a black permanent pen to write *wishing* and *you* in script on the 2" x 2" blue denim cardstock. Cut out each word, making small rectangular tabs no more than $1/2$" high. The exact height and length of the tabs will depend on your penmanship. Draw a thin black line on the $2^3/8$" x $1^1/8$" blue denim cardstock, $1/8$" in from the cut edges all around.

4. Create a computer file and type the word *joy*. To match the project card, use the CK Lumpy font in 72-point (from the CK Fresh Fonts CD). Print the file onto white cardstock. Immediately remove the cardstock from the printer and sprinkle silver embossing powder over the word. Heat with a heat tool to melt the powder and emboss the surface. Allow to cool. (See "Working with Text" on page 8 and "Embossing" on page 7.)

5. Cut out the individual letters made in step 4. Mount the letters on the $2^3/8$" x $1^1/8$" blue denim cardstock, using a tape runner. Let the *j* and *y* descenders overlap the hand-drawn line along the bottom edge.

6. Mount a photo on each metal-rimmed tag, using adhesive tabs. Punch a hole in each photo to match the hole in the tags, using a $1/8$" hole punch. Install pewter eyelets into the photo tags, using a setting tool and a hammer. (See "Installing Eyelets" on page 9.) Thread white string (packaged with tags) through each hole, tie the ends together, and cut off excess.

7. Open the card flat. Punch a hole in the card front, 2" from the left edge and $2^1/2$" from the bottom edge, using a $1/8$" hole punch. Install the *Christmas* eyelet word, using an eyelet setter and a hammer. (See "Installing Eyelets" on page 9.)

8. Lay out the snowflake charm and the collage elements made in steps 3–6 on the card front, as shown in the project photo (page 88). Stamp three snowflakes in tinted embossing ink in the open spaces, using the snowflake rubber stamp. Working quickly, remove the loose collage pieces from the card and sprinkle silver embossing powder over the wet ink. Shake off and conserve the excess powder. Heat with a heat tool to melt the powder and emboss the surface. (See "Embossing" on page 7.)

9. Re-create your step 8 collage layout. Attach the snowflake charm using scrapbook glue. Mount the cardstock pieces with adhesive tabs. Mount the photo tags with glue dots.

Materials (for tree card)

- 8" x $8^1/2$" piece of blue denim cardstock (Archiver's)
- 4" x $4^3/4$" piece of white cardstock (Archiver's)
- 3" x $7^1/2$" piece of light blue pearlescent handmade textured paper (Creative Papers Online)
- 4 to 5 assorted blue handmade paper scraps (Creative Papers Online)
- Star stamp (Stampendous!: #C092)
- Silver embossing powder (Ranger Industries)
- Embossing inkpad (Top Boss)
- *merry christmas* eyelet word (Making Memories)
- 14" length of pom-pom cord (Making Memories: Funky Fibers)
- 14" length of thin silver metallic cord (May Arts)
- 5 blue denim buttons, $1/4$" to $3/8$" diameter (Making Memories)
- Glue dots (Memory Book)
- Double-sided adhesive tabs and dispenser (Centis HERMAfix)
- Photo tape (3M: Scotch Photo & Document Tape)
- pH neutral scrapbook glue (Magic Scraps: Scrappy Glue)
- Basic card-making tools (see page 11)
- 2" x 2" square punch (Creative Memories)
- $1^1/2$" x $1^1/2$" square punch (Creative Memories)
- $1^1/4$" x $1^1/4$" square punch (Creative Memories)
- 1" x 1" square punch (Creative Memories)
- $1/8$" "anywhere" hole punch
- Eyelet setter
- Hammer
- Template plastic
- Heat tool

Instructions
(for tree card)

1. Score and fold the denim cardstock in half to make a 4" x 8½" card, folded edge at left. (See "Folding Paper" on page 5.)

2. Follow the diagram to mark a diagonal line on the white card-stock. Cut on the marked line and discard the triangle. Mount the remaining piece on the card front, longest edge on the fold, using adhesive tabs.

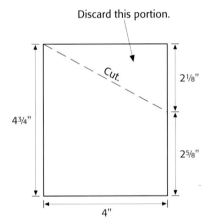

Discard this portion.

Cut.

2⅛"

4¾"

2⅝"

4"

3. Cut 4 squares in graduated sizes from the assorted handmade paper scraps, using the square paper punches. Cut 1 more square using the 1¼" punch.

4. Arrange the squares in size order on the left side of the card, angling them and overlapping the corners, to create a teetering pile of presents. Affix with adhesive tabs. Tie the silver cord into a bow and glue it to the top present, using scrapbook glue.

5. Trace the tree pattern (at right) onto template plastic. Cut out the template. Trace around the template with a pencil to mark 1 tree on pearlescent paper. Cut out the tree. (See "Templates" on page 6.)

6. Hold the silver and pom-pom cords together. Tape the ends to the back of the tree, as close to the top as possible, using photo tape. Wrap both strands loosely around the tree about 6 times, spiraling downward until you reach the base. Trim and tape down the ends on the reverse side. Attach buttons to the tree using glue dots.

7. Stamp a star in embossing ink at the top right corner of the card. Sprinkle silver embossing powder onto the wet ink. Shake off and conserve the excess powder. Heat with a heat tool to melt the powder and emboss the surface. (See "Embossing" on page 7.)

8. Mount the tree on the card front, with the embossed star at the top, using adhesive tabs.

9. Open the card flat. Punch a hole in the center of the card front, using a ⅛" hole punch. Install the *merry christmas* eyelet word, using an eyelet setter and a hammer. (See "Installing Eyelets" on page 9.)

Tree Pattern

FISHERMAN'S BIRTHDAY CARDS 🪶

By Sonya Anderson
Instructor for Archiver's—
The Photo Memory Store

Materials (for photos card)

- 6½" x 11" piece of gray cardstock
- 2¼" x 2¼" piece of dark brown cardstock with torn edges
- 2¾" x 3" piece of heavily textured handmade paper (Creative Papers Online)
- 2½" x 8½" piece of brown self-adhesive mesh (Advant Card: Magic Mesh)
- 3" x 3" sepia-tone bare feet photo
- 1¾" x 1¾" sepia-tone fish photo
- Fishing lure sticker (EK Success: Fresh Stickers)

- 3½" novelty fishing pole (EK Success: Jolee's By You)
- Circle alphabet charms (Making Memories)
- Printer's uppercase alphabet stamps (Hero Arts)
- Black dye-based inkpad
- Red metallic fibers (EK Success: Adornments)
- Double-sided adhesive tabs and dispenser (Centis HERMAfix)
- pH neutral scrapbook glue (Magic Scraps: Scrappy Glue)
- Basic card-making tools (see page 11)

Let him know that you know how much he loves fishing. Embellishments for this pair of masculine theme birthday cards include a mesh net, fish hooks and lures, a catch-of-the-day photo, and a miniature rod. A paper fish swims along in the rippling waters of a handmade paper.

Instructions (for photos card)

1. Score and fold the gray cardstock in half to make a 5½" x 6½" card, folded edge at left. (See "Folding Paper" on page 5.)

2. Cut the handmade paper diagonally in half to make two triangles. Align and mount one triangle on the upper left corner of the card front, using adhesive tabs. Mount the bare feet photo below the triangle, angling it so the top left corner of the photo almost touches the card's folded edge and the bottom left corner of the photo almost touches the bottom edge.

3. Open the card flat. Place self-adhesive mesh on card front, parallel to and ¼" from right edge of card. Fold excess mesh at top and bottom edges to back side.

4. Mount the fish photo on the dark brown cardstock, using adhesive tabs. Mount the layered photo on the card at the top right, angling it so that the top left corner almost touches the card's top edge and the top right corner touches the card's right edge.

5. Glue an uppercase *Y* alphabet charm to the card, 1³/₈" from the left edge and 2¹/₈" from the top edge, using scrapbook glue. Glue three more charms alongside, staggering the distance from the top edge, to spell out *YOUR*. Let the *R* charm overlap the mesh and the fish photo piece.

6. Glue a mini *E* alphabet charm to the card, ³/₄" from the lower edge and 2¹/₈" from the right edge, using scrapbook glue. Glue four more charms alongside, staggering the distance from the lower edge, to spell out *enjoy*.

7. Stamp *IT'S* in black ink above the *YOUR* charms and *DAY* in black ink below the *YOUR* charms, using the printer's alphabet stamps.

8. Apply the lure sticker to the mesh, between the fish photo and the *enjoy* charms. Glue the fishing pole to the card front, as shown in the project photo (page 92), using scrapbook glue. Tie a few red metallic fibers to the fish hook to resemble a fishing fly. Secure the fish hook in the mesh.

Materials (for tag card)

- 8¹/₂" x 11" piece of light blue cardstock
- 3³/₄" x 5¹/₄" piece of dark gray cardstock
- 3¹/₂" x 5" piece of jute cardstock
- 3¹/₂" x 2¹/₂" piece of light gray cardstock
- 2" x 1" piece of light gray cardstock
- 2³/₄" x 3¹/₂" piece of black-and-silver handmade paper (Creative Papers Online)
- Scraps of green, blue, and gray cardstock
- 1"-diameter metal-rimmed white tag (Making Memories)
- Printer's uppercase alphabet stamps (Hero Arts)
- Black dye-based inkpad
- Computer and printer
- Extra computer fonts (CK Fresh Fonts CD)
- Circle alphabet charms (Making Memories)
- Random alphabet charms (Making Memories)
- Silver oval-shaped clip (Making Memories)
- ³/₁₆" pewter eyelet (Making Memories)
- Two ¹/₈" pewter eyelets (Making Memories)

- 24-gauge black spool wire (Artistic Wire Ltd.)
- Green yarn (Making Memories: Funky Fibers)
- 11" lengths of several fibers (EK Success: Adornments)
- Double-sided adhesive tabs and dispenser (Centis HERMAfix)
- Foam adhesive dots (All Night Media: Mini Pop Dots)
- pH neutral scrapbook glue (Magic Scraps: Scrappy Glue)
- Glue dots (Memory Book)
- Basic card-making tools (see page 11)
- ⁷/₈" circle cutter (Creative Memories)
- ¹/₂" circle punch
- ³/₁₆" hole punch
- ¹/₈" hole punch
- Jewelry pliers
- Round-nose pliers
- Eyelet setter
- Hammer
- Template plastic

Instructions (for tag card)

1. Trace tag patterns A and B (page 95) onto template plastic. Cut out both templates. Punch a hole in template A using a ³/₁₆" hole punch. (See "Templates" on page 6.)

2. Align template A on the jute cardstock. Mark the corner angles and the hole circle, using a pencil. Align template B on the dark gray cardstock. Mark the corner angles. Trim off all the corners as marked. Cut a circle from the dark gray waste cardstock, using a ¹/₂" circle punch.

3. Center and mount the jute tag on the dark gray tag, using adhesive tabs. Mount the dark gray circle over the marked hole circle. Punch a hole at that spot through all three layers, using a ³/₁₆" hole punch. Install a ³/₁₆" pewter eyelet, using an eyelet setter and a hammer. (See "Installing Eyelets" on page 9.) Hitch the 11" fibers through the eyelet hole.

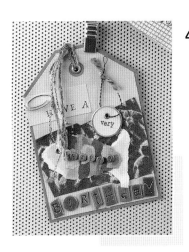

4. Stamp the words *HAVE A* in black ink on the 1" x 2" light gray cardstock, using the uppercase alphabet stamps. To match the look on the project card, work backwards, starting with an *A* at the lower right corner. Mount the stamped piece on the card, just below the angled cut and flush with the left edge, using adhesive tabs. Slip an oval clip onto the left edge.

5. Arrange random alphabet charms across the bottom of the card to spell out *Birthday*. Adhere the charms with scrapbook glue.

6. Cut into the 3¹/₂" edges of the handmade paper with scissors to make jagged contours. Test-fit the paper on the card between *HAVE A* and *Birthday*, aligning the short edges on the jute cardstock. Trim the short edges at an angle to reveal more of the jute cardstock underneath. Mount the paper on the card, using adhesive tabs.

7. Tear the 3¹/₂" x 2¹/₂" light gray cardstock into a fish shape about 3" long. Tear the assorted cardstock scraps into small pieces, about ³/₈" x ¹/₂". Glue the pieces to the fish with scrapbook glue, overlapping them to suggest fish scales. Glue small circle charms to the fish gills to spell *happy*. Allow to dry.

8. Punch a hole in the fish for an eye, using a ¹/₈" hole punch. Install a pewter ¹/₈" eyelet, using an eyelet setter and a hammer. (See "Installing Eyelets" on page 9.) Mount the fish on the card, above the word *Birthday*, using adhesive tabs.

9. Create a computer file and type the word *very*. To match the project card, use the CK Corral font (from the CK Fresh Fonts CD) in 14-point. Print the file onto light blue cardstock. (See "Working with Text" on page 8.)

10. Cut out the printed word, using a ⁷/₈" circle cutter. Mount the circle on the metal-rimmed tag, using a paper-thin adhesive dot. Punch a hole in the tag, using a ¹/₈" hole punch. Install a ¹/₈" pewter eyelet, using an eyelet setter and a hammer. (See "Installing Eyelets" on page 9.)

11. Cut a 7" length of wire. Bend the wire in half. Grasp and crimp the two cut ends together, using jewelry pliers. Grasp the looped end with round-nose pliers. Twist to spiral the wires together along the entire length. Bend the cut end into a hook shape. Tie a 5" piece of yarn ¹/₂" below the open loop. Trim the yarn tails to ¹/₂".

12. Slip the round tag from step 10 onto the hook. Mount the hook and tag on the card, as shown in the project photo (at left), using scrapbook glue for the hook and a glue dot for the tag.

B

A

Tag Patterns

SOURCES

The craft products featured in this book are available online and at craft and art supply retailers nationwide. Contact the vendors listed here for additional information.

Archiver's—The Photo Memory Store
6440 Flying Cloud Dr. Suite 135
Eden Prairie, MN 55344
877-867-7857
www.archiversonline.com
Visit the Web site for an informative guide to scrapbooking, photo, and memorabilia preservation supplies. Directory of retail stores in Colorado, Illinois, Minnesota, and Wisconsin.

Clearsnap, Inc.
888-448-4862
www.clearsnap.com
Twelve different inkpad brands, Top Boss embossing supplies, rubber stamps. Fun Web site includes product demos. Online ordering.

Creative Imaginations
www.cigift.com
View scrapbooking paper and sticker collections online. Directory of online retailers plus a retail store locator.

Creative Papers Online
800-727-3740
handmade-paper.us
Handmade paper (1,700 varieties), mulberry paper, metallic paper, cardstock, vellum, note cards, skeleton leaves, embellishments, and collage packs. Online ordering.

Dick Blick
800-828-4548
info@dickblick.com
www.dickblick.com
Extensive paper selection, plus paper edgers, punches, adhesives, art supplies to order online.

Dover Publications
store.doverpublications.com
Copyright-free art to order online.

Hero Arts
www.heroarts.com
Read articles on stamping techniques and tips. View sophisticated product line of rubber stamps, inks, and completed projects. Store locator by zip code.

Impress Rubber Stamps
www.impressrubberstamps.com
Rubber stamps, inkpads, note cards, paper, eyelets, charms, punches, ribbon, tools to order online. Lots of collage cards to give you ideas.

Magic Scraps
972-238-1838
www.magicscraps.com
All types of scrapbook embellishments—fibers, eyelets, metal accents, tags, mesh, ribbon—plus adhesives and tools to order online. Gallery of scrapbooking ideas, plus a tips and techniques section.

Making Memories
www.makingmemories.com
Stickers, paper, tags, metal accents. Some items available through the online shop. For others, locate a store near you by zip code. Sample cards offer great ideas.

Memory Box
888-723-1484
www.memoryboxco.com
Cards, cardstock, scrapbook papers, and rubber stamps.

Paper Addict
paperaddict.com
All types of paper to order online, including Anna Griffin, Autumn Leaves, Debbie Mumm, Magenta, 7 Gypsies. You can also shop for stickers, brads, clips, glue dots, and HERMAfix dots and tabs.

PSX
800-782-6748
www.psxdesign.com
Over 4,000 rubber stamps, stickers, plus a full line of stamping accessories, including inks, paper, tools, and embellishments. Order online, request a catalog, or use the zip code search to find a store near you. Find out about rubber stamping events, too.

Rio Grande
800-545-6566
www.riogrande.com
A source for the steel bench block, used to make the Valentine's Day Cards (page 17).

Savvy Stamps
360-993-3802
savvystamps@savvystamps.com
www.savvystamps.com
Distinctive rubber stamps, striped note cards, rhinestones, paper flowers to order online. Clean, easy-to-navigate Web site.